LOYALTY

PAYS

LOYALTY PAYS

A HISTORY OF THE UNITED CLUBS BREWERY

BRIAN GLOVER

ALAN SUTTON PUBLISHING LIMITED
in association with
CROWN BUCKLEY

First published in the United Kingdom in 1995
Alan Sutton Publishing Ltd · Phoenix Mill · Far Thrupp · Stroud · Gloucestershire

Copyright © Brian Glover, 1995

All rights reserved. No part of this publication may be reproduced, stored in a retrieval system, or transmitted, in any form, or by any means, electronic, mechanical, photocopying, recording or otherwise, without the prior permission of the publishers and copyright holder.

British Library Cataloguing in Publication Data
Glover, Brian
  Loyalty Pays: History of the United Clubs
  Brewery
  I. Title
  338.7663309429

ISBN 0-7509-0832-7

Typeset in 11/13 Perpetua.
Typesetting and origination by
Alan Sutton Publishing Limited.
Printed in Great Britain by
Ebenezer Baylis, Worcester.

Contents

Foreword	vii
Preface	ix
Clubbing Together	1
Own Brew	9
Surviving the Slump, 1919–1929	18
Beating the Depression, 1930–1939	31
Heart of the Community	42
Battle Stations, 1939–1945	49
Building Hopes, 1945–1954	59
Champion Years, 1955–1966	72
Fighting the Giants, 1967–1976	86
Uneasy Crown, 1977–1988	105
Crown Buckley, 1988–1994	124
Stout Rescues, 1990–1994	137
Index	144

FOREWORD

In June 1993 Crown Buckley was the subject of a management buyout – the latest in a long series of events to overtake the companies making up Crown Buckley. This business was formed in 1989 by the merger of two South Wales brewers: Buckleys, a traditional family brewer dating back to the eighteenth century (Wales' oldest brewery) and Crown Brewery, formerly the United Clubs Brewery. Clearly Buckleys had the longer history, but this book celebrates a unique and brave enterprise, the United Clubs Brewery at Pontyclun.

It was founded in 1919 by a committee formed from the CIU clubs in South Wales, none of whom had any previous experience of running a brewery. This book chronicles the remarkable story of the brewery at Pontyclun up to the present day.

The buyout in 1993 was yet a further chapter in the history of this company and would not have been contemplated without the full support of the clubs and shareholders in the old company. Although control of the company has changed hands it is still very much a 'clubs' brewery relying greatly on the clubs – its area of great strength. Many of those clubs are still shareholders. Their loyalty throughout this period of change has been noteworthy and many of our present-day club customers were founder members of the brewery in 1919.

There is a sad lack of pictures and memorabilia relating to the brewery (due in part I am sure to the many changes that have taken place over the years) but there is a full set of minute books from the very beginning to the present day. These are not the usual dry record of business but give a very detailed portrait of the brewery over the years. These, coupled with personal reminiscences, form the bulk of the material that Brian Glover has so skilfully put together to create this book.

I would like to express my gratitude to him for providing such a worthy history to celebrate the seventy-fifth anniversary of the brewery. I am also most grateful to all those who came forward and supplied material and their own memories.

Finally, I would like to thank all those customers, employees and others who have contributed to the brewery's past and continue to contribute to its present and future. This book is dedicated to them all.

Mike Salter
Managing Director

PREFACE

When Mike Salter, the managing director of Crown Buckley, asked me to write this book, I thought it would just be a matter of expanding the chapter on the South Wales and Monmouthshire United Clubs Brewery which appeared in my book *Prince of Ales, The History of Brewing in Wales*.

Then Mike turned up at my home with an estate car full of weighty minute books and a huge black trunk packed with company papers. I had a mountain of original material to scale as my house turned into a mini-archive.

Hopefully, I have managed to pull a coherent story from this mass of detail; a story about a unique co-operative enterprise which has never been told before.

I would like to thank all the staff and workers at Crown Buckley who have helped with my research, and the staff of the Club and Institute Union who were also eager to assist.

Brian Glover

HEART OF THE BEER: Brewhouse worker Charles Slawson prepares to pour a bag of malt down the chute at the brewery in 1969

CLUBBING TOGETHER

THE EARLY CIU MOVEMENT

Clubs are as old as pubs. Arranged along trade or political lines, they existed in ancient Greece and the Roman Empire. Some wit even suggested that the caveman's club was not a hefty branch of oak, but that snug cavern round the corner where the men of the tribe gathered to discuss the next day's hunting over a bison steak and a jug of fermented juice.

Clubs particularly flourished in London. Dr Samuel Johnson – who in his lifetime was also the director of a prominent brewery – wrote 'the great chair of a full and pleasant town club is, perhaps, the throne of human felicity'. But these clubs were for the prominent and the prosperous. As in many other aspects of life, the working man had little or nothing. As a miner complained to the *Merthyr Express* after the closing of pubs in Wales on Sunday: 'These very generous people have their nice cosy clubs . . . but the collier has to live in discomfort in a small house and for near six months in every year never sees the sun.'

The Friendly Societies from the eighteenth century were worthy organizations, offering security against old age, sickness and adversity. But they tended to be closed, conservative, middle class bodies, usually meeting in private rooms in pubs. Labourers were rarely welcome. The societies did not seek men without a trade who might be a heavy drain on resources because of their uncertain employment.

Not a single member of the Welsh Lodges of Oddfellows, for instance, was involved in the rebellion in the coalfields and the iron industry which led to the shooting of twenty-six workers by troops in Merthyr Tydfil in 1831 and the execution of one of the leaders, Dic Penderyn. Indeed, the Druids and Oddfellows offered the services of their entire membership as special constables as the unrest grew in 1830.

But some members of the privileged classes were concerned about the plight of labourers, as vividly exposed in Charles Dickens' novels. They were mainly clergymen or other high-minded individuals who were appalled by the suffering caused by the industrial revolution. As slums and squalor spread, they felt something had to be done to save the working man. They were less concerned for his physical welfare than his moral and religious standing. They were imbued with the earnest but rather vague intention of 'elevating' the working classes. Above all, most were firm temperance reformers. The factory hands and miners had to be rescued from the degradation of drink, not provided with better facilities in which to enjoy a relaxing pint at the end of the day.

They were looking for a dry alternative to the perils of the pub. Education was seen as vital. Dr Birkbeck led a movement to set up mechanics' institutes and reading rooms.

Mutual improvement societies were established, usually meeting in schools, to provide classes or discussions. A Manchester curate wrote a pamphlet suggesting the formation of clubs for working men. It was read by one of the most remarkable men of the century, Revd Henry Solly, a Unitarian minister in Yeovil, Somerset. A keen supporter of the Chartists, he seized on the idea with enthusiasm. He went to London determined to set up a national organization. Against overwhelming odds, he cajoled the support of many leading men of the day. Lord Brougham accepted the presidency, and the list of vice-presidents included six peers. He almost persuaded the future Prime Minister William Gladstone to become a vice-president and squeezed a donation of 20 guineas out of the Prince of Wales.

At its first meeting in June 1862, the Working Men's Club and Institute Union, as it was called, pledged to pepper the country with clubs. These were to be places where working men 'can meet for conversation, business and mental improvement, with the means of recreation and refreshment, free from intoxicating drinks'. There was to be no beer. 'Recreation must go hand in hand with education and temperance.'

Solly believed this was the wish of the working man: 'While the union is altogether independent of the total abstinence movement it aims especially at forming clubs in which intoxicating drinks shall not be admitted,' he wrote in a pamphlet. 'The workmen themselves are most anxious to have their clubs free from what they feel to be so great an evil at the public house. Fifty years hence it may be different. But I am quite sure that, for a long time to come, working men will tell us that a fundamental rule in all such clubs should be the total exclusion of intoxicating drink.' This firm belief was soon swept away by a tide of beer and spirits.

By the end of the first twelve months, Solly, who was secretary of the new organisation, had helped set up or affiliated fifty-three working men's clubs across England. He toured the country and poured out pamphlets and letters to newspapers. Temperance workers and those eager to better themselves joined up. There was just one problem. The working man, conspicuous by his absence, showed little interest in the clubs built for his benefit. Many quickly closed.

The movement swiftly realized the problem. Working men liked a pipe (smoking was also banned) and a pint after hours of toil. One of the vice-presidents of the CIU, Lord Lyttleton, protested about the restrictions, and at a special meeting in 1863 it was agreed to rescind the ban in favour of a 'recommendation' that clubs keep liquor off the premises.

But the leaders still frowned on a glass of beer and did all they could to keep the cask out of the club. Solly strongly advised one man who inquired about setting up an institute in Leicester in 1865 to exclude all ale, telling him the tall tale of the club which introduced beer, 'but there was so little demand that it became sour before the cask was finished, and proved to be too expensive a luxury'.

As clubs followed the union line, so a growing number closed. Emergency conferences were called to investigate the problem and concluded that clubs must sell beer to survive. Even Solly was converted. He admitted 'what had not generally been realized by the earlier promoters of the movement, that there is a very large number of respectable working men who desire to have a pint of beer after the day's work is done . . . and if they cannot get it at their club they will go for it elsewhere'.

SHARP ATTACK: The power of the prohibition lobby seriously alarmed the commercial brewers during the nineteenth century, prompting them to print pamphlets like this warning drinkers to be on their guard against the 'teetotal fanatics'

The seal was set on the new policy at the annual meeting of the CIU in 1868. The President, the Earl of Caernarfon, told the delegates: 'A question which has excited a good deal of feeling and discussion amongst clubs both in London and the country, and one which has caused a division of opinion, is how far it is prudent to allow the introduction of alcoholic liquors. If the introduction of beers and spirits were to lead to excess, there is no friend of the institutions who would not deeply deplore it. On the other hand, if these institutions were really to be rivals to and substitutes for the public house, then the introduction of such articles of consumption under prudent regulations might be very wise. It is a matter to be determined entirely by the good sense of the working man.'

The movement was growing up. Instead of ordering clubs what to do, the founding fathers were at last treating working men like adults, and allowing them to decide their own rules. As Solly admitted, 'I do not wish to see working men treated like children. There should be no interference by persons outside.' The teetotal supporters were routed.

Some clubs were cautious with their new freedom. Hoddlesden reported: 'Smoking is allowed and beer allowed, limited to one pint. So far it has answered admirably.' So admirably that by 1894 the Lancashire club had emptied the village pub. That year the landlord refused to pay rent unless the Lady of the Manor closed the club.

Northampton Working Men's Club reported in 1873: 'When first started we began the wrong way, allowing only coffee, tea and ginger beer. Young lads used to be the principal members and men won't associate with boys. Since we have altered our rules and allowed the beer, we have what may be called the cream of the working men.'

Batley Working Men's in Yorkshire reported in 1876: 'Since we introduced beer into our club we have made wonderful progress, both in finance and numbers. We have nothing to regret, but everything to rejoice for. Of course, all extreme teetotallers have left, but we have a few reasonable temperance men left with us yet. We claim to be the real temperance reformers because, unlike the extremists, we lay hold of the masses of the people.'

One of the CIU's leaders, Hodgson Pratt, summed up the new position: 'We must not have one law for the rich and another for the poor in this matter. I would be ashamed to take it for granted that no artisans could be trusted to take beer or spirits in moderation. I believe that the substitution of clubs for public houses – which can only be done by allowing beer in the clubs – will make the nation temperate.'

Following this crucial change of policy, the number of CIU clubs supplying alcohol rose steadily. From a quarter in 1874, those with booze at the bar swelled to 41 per cent in 1878 and 79 per cent in 1883. By 1921 98 per cent of the 2,149 clubs served their members beer and spirits. As B.T. Hall, secretary of the CIU from 1893 to 1929, said in his book *Our Sixty Years*, recording the movement's first six decades in 1922, 'It is difficult to see how any other conclusion could have been reached. For whether teetotalism be good or bad it is not a basis on which a workmen's club can be reared. It was plain to the many, who accepted the fact with reluctance, that if beer was prohibited there would soon be neither clubs nor union.' The movement had recognized that 'the great majority of the best and foremost workmen still consider beer an indispensable adjunct to social life'.

Hall believed this decision had done more to promote moderate drinking than all the

CLOSE COMPANIONS: *The early CIU might have banned beer, but the movement soon went pint in hand. By 1937, though the Club and Institute's magazine still carried the temperance slogan on its masthead, the union was quite happy to carry 'Beer is Best' advertising from the Brewers' Society on its front cover*

strident efforts of the prohibition parties. 'Rare is now the workman who is drunk without shame.' The clubs provided a relaxed and controlled environment for enjoying a pint, weaning the workman 'by discipline and honour from violence and excess'.

'In those districts where workmen's clubs are the most numerous and oldest established there drunkenness is found at its minimum. In districts where they have hitherto been unknown, their introduction has worked a revolution. Nowhere amongst workmen is there so potent an agency against drunkenness as the workmen's clubs.'

Brewers, of course, who were investing heavily in their own tied houses, did not view clubs in the same light. Many were deeply suspicious of these rival outlets which were beyond their control – and for many years outside government legislation. Clubs were undefined and had no system of registration until the Licensing Act of 1902. In South Wales the atmosphere was particularly chilly. Miners and other industrial workers who had flooded into the area during the nineteenth century, often into remote, isolated places in the valleys, had sought security in working men's clubs and welfare institutes. Most of these were smaller than their English counterparts, and few were members of the CIU. In fact the South Wales branch of the CIU was not formed until 1909, and two years later major towns like Swansea and Merthyr Tydfil still had no affiliated clubs.

The number of clubs had sharply increased after the Sunday Closing (Wales) Act of 1881 which, much to the brewers' wrath, shut pubs on the holy day but allowed clubs to stay open. Some of the clubs set up at this time were little more than illicit drinking dens (shebeens). The brewers were not amused by the way they evaded the growing restrictions placed on pubs. Samuel Brain of the famous Cardiff brewers sharply expressed their anger when he gave evidence before the Royal Commission looking into the working of the Act in 1889: 'I could give you numbers of instances where men have gone into clubs and shebeens and places of that description on a Saturday night after they have finished their work, and have not come out of them until Monday, and they spend their wages and mix with low society and all that sort of thing, which was never the case when they could get their dinner beer (in a pub) on the Sunday and stop at home.'

Many of these clubs, especially in large towns like Cardiff, were private premises where men gathered to satisfy one common need – a thirst on Sunday. Samuel Brain told the commission how they operated: 'The great majority of the private houses in certain districts here have in immense quantities of beer on Saturday nights, and in fact right up to one or two o'clock in the morning. It was nothing unusual for the well-conducted licensed victualler to stand at his door on Saturday nights, after he has closed his premises at 11 o'clock, and see brewers' drays and agents' carts delivering seventy or eighty small casks into private houses within 100 yards of his premises.'

Though such places were not typical of the miners' clubs up the valleys, they further soured the strained relationship between brewers and clubs. There was little love and less trust. The authorities were also obstructive, with magistrates and police generally trying to oppose the growth of clubs in South Wales, which they believed were just trying to evade the licensing laws.

In 1883, eighteen months after the passing of the Sunday Closing Act, the chief constable of Cardiff reported that twelve official clubs had been established with 2,854 members. And many more shifty establishments were springing up. He had to admit to the watch committee that he had no power to control them. More embarrassingly for him, the committee had to deal with police constables drinking in these clubs.

Only after a successful prosecution in Bristol in 1886 was effective action taken in Cardiff to suppress clubs 'of a bogus character', with 130 being prosecuted or forced to close down between July and November that year. By 1898 the chief constable was able to report that 'there are now thirty clubs in Cardiff, none actually bogus though some few were of a shady character'.

Cardiff's extreme experience was repeated to a lesser degree throughout industrial South Wales. By the end of the century better-run clubs had become an established part of society, with crude drinking dens largely suppressed except in Barry, where the docks developed late. Cardiff's chief constable in 1910 told the watch committee that clubs were generally 'well conducted and few breaches of the law arise from them. Indeed clubs are much more carefully managed of late years, than they were fifteen or twenty years ago.'

There were always exceptions, and some used respected names to mask their true activities. Abergwynfi Conservative Club was prosecuted at Aberavon in 1905 for being nothing more than a boozers' shop, operating a very generous slate system. There was even a free drinks book which the prosecution solicitor 'refrained from showing the bench as it might make them envious'. The club could not afford to send a representative to a Tory rally in Pontypridd, but the following Friday passed a resolution that 'all members get free drinks'. The prosecution concluded that 'such a club prostituted the name of one of the great parties of the country in order to carry on illicit drinking'.

Cases like this kept cropping up, but many politicians viewed clubs as possible sources of support, and were unlikely to back widespread action against them. Even the Liberal Party, which keenly pursued prohibition policies, drew the line at curbing clubs. *The Times* in 1909, commenting on the Liberal Government's anti-drink budget, claimed the party was biased in favour of clubs. 'The impression, now fairly general, is that publicans are to be punished because they are not supposed to be friends of the Liberal Party, while clubs are to be favoured because they are frequently found very useful as centres of Liberal propaganda.'

While those in authority might be more at ease, the brewers still deeply resented these barely restricted rivals to their public houses. Their attitude was not helped by the number of clubs going out of business leaving heavy debts. Blaengarw Constitutional Club folded owing Pontyclun beer merchant Thomas Morgan £500 on a loan account and £622 on a trading account. These were considerable sums in 1906.

But clubs were becoming more organized. After the formation of the South Wales branch of the CIU in 1909, with thirty-four clubs affiliated within three years, one of the early acts of the energetic secretary, J.W. Kinsman, was to establish an audit department in 1913 to help clubs organize their finances.

The branch proved a powerful lobby for the clubs movement in the region – and a forceful focus for joint action. Money began to be collected to build a convalescent home at Langland Bay near Swansea. Around £1,200 had been raised by 1914 when the First World War intervened and brought more pressing problems. Minister of Munitions Lloyd George had long supported prohibition, and he was to use the conflict to introduce draconian restrictions on the supply of alcohol. 'We are fighting Germany, Austria and the drink,' he declared in one wartime speech. 'And as far as I can see the greatest of these deadly foes is drink.' Under the Defence of the Realm Act (DORA) pub – and club – opening hours were slashed. In some areas like Carlisle breweries were taken over and all were severely restricted in the amount they could produce. Beer taxation soared. The price of a pint followed. Buying a round was banned.

Naturally the breweries distributed the limited supply of beer to their own pubs first. Clubs were left high and dry. Resentment mounted – and a growing number of club members began to believe that the only solution was to establish their own brewery.

Own Brew

The friction between clubs and brewers during the First World War was not just about supply, but also concerned the quality of the beer produced under wartime restrictions – and its ever-rising price. This was reflected in a motion of the South Wales branch of the CIU at Abercarn in December 1916: 'That in the opinion of this branch the action of the brewers in raising their prices by such a large amount, having regard to the fact that they have been obtaining sums over and above the increase in taxation since November 1914, is entirely unwarranted and unnecessary.'

Clubs believed they were being ripped off. They were correct. For brewers made good money on their restricted sales of much weaker (and therefore cheaper to produce) but higher-priced beers.

Professors Richard Wilson and Terry Gourvish in their study of the British brewing industry said about the First World War: 'The later war years and immediate post-war period were good ones for brewers. They were allowed to advance prices significantly as duties rose sharply, and since an Excess Profits Duty was introduced rather late and less tightly than in 1939, brewers enjoyed extremely healthy profits on their reduced sales. Their weak, characterless beers sold readily.'

The CIU clubs in South Wales were not impressed by the product, the price or the poor service. They determined to do something about it, once the war was over. A sub-committee, appointed in 1918 to investigate the possibility of brewing their own beer, included many of the men who were to take the project through to fermentation and beyond – J.P. Davies, A. Pearce, T. Rich, H.T. Richards, H. Howe and the South Wales branch secretary, J.W. Kinsman. A formal motion adopting the policy was carried at a representative meeting of clubs at the Cathays Liberal Club in Cardiff on 28 March 1919, and no time was lost in setting the barrel rolling. In May the brewery sub-committee reported that they were 'now in a position to acquire a brewery on behalf of the South Wales clubs'. Members of the CIU offered to subscribe £22,000 towards the scheme.

The brewery the club collective had in its sights was D.&T. Jenkins' Crown Brewery at Pontyclun, with an output of 400 barrels a week. The brothers David and Thomas, whose family were brewers in Cowbridge to the south, had built the tall stone brewhouse at the beginning of the century on a strategic site alongside the Cowbridge to Llantrisant road at Brynsadler, Pontyclun. The Vale of Glamorgan, centred on the old market town of Cowbridge, was a quietly prosperous rural area, dominated by farming. The growing market for beer was to the north, in the steep coal-blackened mining valleys. Pontyclun was the gateway to the valleys, with roads running to the Rhondda.

The brothers' company, D.&T. Jenkins Ltd, had been registered in 1902 with a capital of £10,000. Though they came to own a number of pubs – Thomas Jenkins was the landlord of the Ivor Arms opposite the brewery – their main business was supplying working men's clubs in the mining valleys with Crown Pale Ale and XXXX. So the business was already ready-made for the clubmen.

On 17 June 1919 a meeting at the South Wales CIU offices in Taff Street, Pontypridd, decided to take an option on the plant and premises at Pontyclun – the pubs were not wanted – and a new company, the South Wales and Monmouthshire United Clubs Brewery was formed with J.P. Davies of Ferndale, a colliery fireman, as chairman. Two months later he was replaced by insurance manager Huw Richards of Pontypridd who was to hold the post for twenty years. The other two original directors were H. Howe of Risca and T. Rich, a Cardiff engineer.

Only CIU clubs and their members could be involved. The South Wales branch by this time numbered sixty-one clubs with over 20,000 members. Directors were appointed to represent both the clubs and the individual shareholders. The discount the clubs received on their beer depended on the size of their shareholding. Just £25,000 was needed to form the company and buy the brewery, though a further £15,000 worth of shares was issued the following year to finance expansion. Nearly 500 applications were received: 45 clubs were issued with 16,240 shares while 445 individuals took 23,760. Of the individual shareholders, 110 applications were for the minimum shareholding of £1.

Since D.&T. Jenkins were already supplying clubs with beer they liked, the new company could begin trading immediately they bought the business on 13 July. They even paid the Jenkins brothers royalties on the beers as head brewer Captain W. Rogers, a cavalry officer in the Boer War, was told to copy the Jenkins' brews. He first produced the dark mild, XXXX, which was described as a 6d beer (for a quart) and sold at £5 a barrel. CPA or Clubs Pale Ale was not introduced until February 1920 at 4s more per barrel.

The reaction of the established brewers to the brave venture was predictable – and hostile. Already struggling to remove the severe regulations imposed during the First World War and worried by the threat of nationalization and the danger of prohibition spreading from the United States, they were in no mood to welcome a new rival. *The Brewers' Journal* of July 1919 reflected the industry's view, a lengthy editorial in the magazine pouring scorn on the development.

'In view of the altered brewing conditions [the Government had just decided to abolish the Central Control Board and remove restrictions on the quantity of beer which could be brewed], the South Wales miners, who have just taken possession of the Crown Brewery at Llantrisant, Glamorgan, after paying the capital sum of £20,000, must be looking askance at those who led them into this venture.

'It was stated that their reason for becoming purchasers was that they found it impossible otherwise to obtain an adequate supply of beer in Rhondda Valley clubs; hence the forming of the company styled the South Wales Club and Institute Union. The upshot of it all is that they have paid this considerable sum to provide themselves with a scarce commodity which has since been made free [of restrictions on quantity].

'The whole scheme seems to be plastered with ineptitude. No man taking thought can add a cubit to his stature. And, as the position was at the date of their purchase, no body of men taking over a brewery could add to their beer supply, for the reason that every barrel of beer permitted to be brewed was brewed, and in 1915–16 the brewery in question was serving customers whose rights of supply remained intact.

CAPTIVATING CROWN: *For a small village brewery before the First World War, D.&J. Jenkins' Crown Brewery at Brynsadler, near Pontyclun, was surprisingly frequently photographed. This was because the enterprising brothers used postcards featuring the brewhouse and their horse-drawn drays to help sell their beers. This simple form of marketing obviously worked. The earliest pictures from 1904 onwards show just one tall tower structure but later postcards carrying their telephone number reveal that an extension has been added. The final ones show lorries. This picture gives a closer view of Crown's single stone tower, waiting for a load of malt*

The earliest postcard dated 1904, produced as part of The Strand Series

The brewery showing new stables, proudly proclaiming their celebrated Crown PA, XXXX and Stout, with an extension to the brewhouse on the left

A postcard clearly showing the extended brewery. Business was booming

'The miners' intention was "to brew a beer from pure malt and hops, and supply a perfectly pure beverage at the lowest possible price". Where the materials were to come from and how "pure malt and hops" – whatever that may mean – were to fit in with "the lowest possible price" are points that remain undisclosed.'

The *Journal's* rambling invective reflects the brewers' frustration that, months after the end of a long, hard war, they were still bound by red tape. Restrictions on the quantity of beer that could be brewed might at last be lifted, but the brewers were still severely limited on the quality. The Government continued to insist that an extremely weak beer with a gravity of 1020 should be brewed and sold at 2d a pint. As Colonel Gretton, MP and chairman of the giant Burton brewers Bass, Ratcliff and Gretton, told the *Weekly Dispatch* in an interview in August 1919: 'When there is a cool weekend there is plenty of weak, washy beer left about the country, which the public does not want to buy and the publicans find most difficult to sell. This is the beer which few people drink so long as they can get anything better, but it is the beer which the Government forces brewers to brew by their foolish and unnecessary restriction upon quality.'

The brewers felt this 'washy beer' was weakening their grip on the public's taste. Sales of wines and spirits were rising. It was also encouraging clubs and landlords to consider brewing their own. The *Brewers' Journal* editorial on the creation of the South Wales clubs concern tried to dismiss this development, but it was spreading across the country.

'It may be remembered that a little prior to the war a similar venture to supply clubs was started by the clubmen in the North of England. It failed. Undeterred by past experience, however, the movement is spreading, and we hear that similar schemes are being prosecuted

A mechanized dray replaces the horse-drawn carts

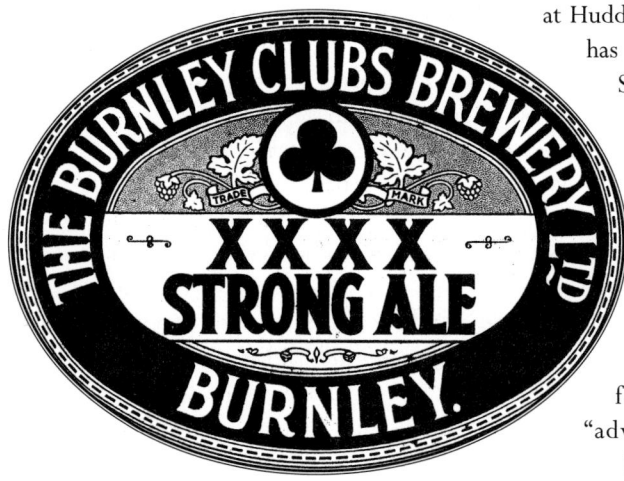

BURNLEY: The first Clubs Brewery in Britain

at Huddersfield, where the Club Union has bought the old Star Brewery at Slaithwaite, and at Bradford, where a proposal is being considered on similar lines.

'Licensed Victuallers, too, it seems, are beset by the same idea of an "independent brewery". The Llandilo local trade association has a motion down for consideration as to the "advisability of purchasing a brewery or the formation of a brewery company, composed of members of the association," while at Bradford off-licence holders are considering a similar scheme. The outcome of these several ventures may, we think, be awaited with equanimity.'

The *Brewers' Journal* might sound confident that all these proposals would fall flat on their faces, but many brewers were concerned that they could steal their business. The failed clubs brewery cited by the *Journal* was the North of England Clubs Brewery registered in 1905 to run the Rainton Brewery at East Rainton between Sunderland and Durham in north-east England. The short-lived company was dissolved in 1909. But the *Journal* failed to mention another company in northern England which did prosper. The Burnley Clubs Brewery was registered in 1901 – the first clubs brewery in Britain – and continued until 1949. A third pre-war venture, the Leeds & District Liberal Clubs Brewery, formed in 1911, went into liquidation two years later, but was revived in 1914 without any political affiliation as the Leeds & District Clubs Brewery. It survived until 1939.

The great wave of clubs breweries, however, arrived after the war. The South Wales and Monmouthshire United Clubs Brewery and the Northern Clubs Federation Brewery of Newcastle led a sudden surge of ventures. After these two were established in 1919, another six appeared in 1920, mainly in the industrial Midlands and North of England. One, the Medway Federation of Clubs Brewery, was set up in Kent.

'The great shortage and the unsatisfactory quality of beer' has prompted workingmen's clubs to investigate the possibility of brewing, reported the *Yorkshire Post* on 23 May 1919. A brewery in Leicester had the support of clubs with a membership of 50–60,000. A subscription of £2 per member, yielding over £100,000, was said to be guaranteed.

The brewing industry was alarmed by the sudden rise of this rival system of co-operative production, not only because it meant more beer on the bar, but because it struck at the heart of the growth area in the market. By the First World War the tied house system was well established. The brewers had bolted up the pub trade. In 1931 the Royal Commission on Licensing estimated that the proportion of on-licences owned by brewers was 'as high as 95 per cent' in England and Wales. It was a mature – and shrinking – market.

Production in the UK in 1913 had been 33.8 million bulk barrels. Between the wars the annual average figure was little more than 24 million. Trade had slumped by at least a quarter. The pub itself was under siege during this period from ardent advocates of improved facilities. The number of publican on-licences fell by 10 per cent from more than 62,000 in 1913 to 56,000 by 1939. The number of off-licences was also slipping.

The only growth area in this depressed picture was the club trade. From 8,738 in 1913, the number of clubs in England and Wales had almost doubled to 17,362 by 1939. Clubs had leaped from 7 to over 15 per cent of the total number of sales outlets. The brewers might grumble about this new competition for their tied houses, but at least it offered the more enterprising a chance to increase their free trade business. That is until the appearance of the clubs' own breweries threatened to snatch this golden opportunity away. The brewers were keenly aware of this marked change in the market, even before the First World War. Their antagonism to clubs – which were less severely regulated than pubs and usually sold beer more cheaply – is clearly shown in another editorial in the *Brewers' Journal* in August 1920:

'The club question, which prior to the war focussed itself so forcibly on brewers in numerous localities, has during the last few months been resuscitated in a somewhat virulent form.

'The official statistics show that the average increase in the number of clubs registered for the sale of alcohol between the years 1905 and 1915 was 230 per annum. During the same period, on-licences and off-licences decreased at an average rate of 1,048 per annum. During the war a number of registered clubs temporarily went out of existence, but there is little doubt that when the statistics for 1919–20 are published, not only will it be found that this decrease has been wiped out, but that the number of clubs is in excess of any previous record.

'How do these clubs exist? We may quote the statement made to one of our correspondents by the secretary of a working men's club (whose receipts for "refreshments" are £8,000 per annum). He said: "Although we do not wish it to be generally known, it is a fact that we are kept going solely by the receipts from our bars. Our subscriptions do not even pay our electric light bill."

'It is common knowledge that the laws governing the restriction of alcohol sales in these institutions are very imperfectly observed. Complaints are rife from licensees that in numerous instances the sale of alcohol in club premises begins at an early hour in the morning and continues beyond the prescribed time at night. . . . The licensee is under the necessity of obeying the restrictions. The same adherence to the law should be enforced in the case of clubs.'

The *Journal* called for the elimination of illegal clubs 'which swell the drunkenness statistics and in which all the evils of excess may be nurtured behind the privacy of the green baize door'. This was the hostile industry into which the new clubs brewery was born. But as long as it was supported by the clubs, it could ignore the jibes from its competitors.

Surviving the Slump

1919–1929

The early years of any enterprise are the most vulnerable. This is particularly true when those in charge have only a limited knowledge of the business. The clubmen knew all about beer when it was in a pint pot – but little about how it got there. Fortunately they were able to lean on the previous owners for advice. The sale had been a friendly transaction and since the Jenkins brothers were being paid royalties on the use of their brews, they were happy to help. In October 1919 David Jenkins was paid to visit Holt Brothers brewery at Burnham in Somerset to inspect and buy further casks. Later he examined vessels in Banbury for the company.

Production started at around 150 barrels a week, with the board eager to press ahead with expansion. Three additional fermenting vessels were added immediately in the brewhouse, 200 casks were bought and Jenkins' horses and carts were replaced by a new four-ton lorry to complement the existing vehicle. This road transport was soon inadequate and warnings were given not to overload the two lorries. Much of the beer was delivered by rail, especially the Taff Vale Railway, and some clubs collected casks themselves from the brewery.

Not everyone was happy with the beer. Ton Pentre club complained about the quality and was asked to send a sample to the brewer; Mountain Ash WMC reported it had lost 18 gallons owing to a cask blowing out. As always, the clubmen put the matter to the vote: 'It was proposed by Mr George Davies, seconded by Mr Dan James, that this club be fully compensated for the loss. An amendment was moved by Mr Howe, seconded by Mr Smith, that the club be compensated to the extent of half the value of the loss. On a vote being taken, the amendment was declared carried.'

Unusually for a brewery, the company operated along co-operative lines. The owners were the retailers. Instead of being for the benefit of the producers, the business was run for the benefit of the customers. The clubs controlled the board. Out of the ten directors, four represented clubs (including the chairman), four represented individual shareholders (who were all club members) and two were co-opted from the executive committee of the South Wales branch of the CIU. The secretary, J.W. Kinsman, was also the secretary of the branch.

Thus the customer was king. This brewery was run from the drinkers' side of the bar. The terms of trade always leaned towards the tippler. They were often generous. Discounts and a merry Christmas bonus were introduced based on the number of barrels bought. Clubs were also given an allowance of one barrel in thirty-six to cover wastage and possible short measure. 'In case of an abnormal shortage the secretary of the club to report the same and the barrel to remain undisturbed to enable a representative of the brewery to inspect same.' The club stewards must have been smiling. It was a system open to abuse.

Though without training, the directors closely supervised the brewing, firing off regular instructions to the brewer: 'Resolved that the secretary write to the brewer instructing him to keep a record of all beer returned.' 'Resolved that the secretary be instructed to prepare forms for the brewer to fill up giving particulars of each brew.' Two of the ten directors attended the brewery every week on a rota basis.

Sub-committees and working committees proliferated and much time was spent discussing directors' fees and allowances. A building committee was established to consider a bold scheme to build their own offices, club premises and bonded store in Mill Street, Pontypridd, next to the County Hotel. The site alone cost £1,100.

They were worried by the water supply to the brewery 'which owing to the long drought had been giving considerable trouble and keeping down the output'. Again they sought David Jenkins' advice, and again appointed another working group, the water and boiler sub-committee. Everything was considered in full democratic detail.

'Resolved that the premises be painted. Proposed by Mr George Davies, seconded by Mr D. Jones, that the name of the company be substituted wherever the name of the old firm appears. An amendment was moved by Mr A. Pearce, seconded by Mr H. Howe, that the name of the company be painted in one place only. On a vote being taken, four voted for the amendment and five for the proposition. The proposition was declared carried.' The board resolved that the name to be displayed was 'Clubs Union Brewery' rather than the cumbersome full title. This name was also painted on the lorries. However, the CIU quickly objected, causing the brushes to hit the brickwork again. The reworded title came out as 'United Clubs Brewery'.

More embarrassingly for a working men's organization, the brewery workers were not happy with their pay. They downed tools and called in Mr Hall, secretary of the Workers Union, just before Christmas. The board responded by appointing a wages sub-committee to meet him. 'The committee were instructed to ask the men to return to work at once with a guarantee that the question of wages would be gone into.' Feelings were running high on the board with some sensing betrayal. 'A discussion took place as to the discipline existing at the brewery and the control of the men employed, and there was a strong expression of opinion that a foreman should be appointed by the board who was thoroughly in sympathy with the main objects of the movement.' This resulted in one of the directors, T. Rich, being appointed foreman at £5 a week, plus a free season ticket from Cardiff to Pontyclun. He retired from the board. At the same time the consideration of an increase in wages was deferred, though members of the wages sub-committee were voted 15s each for attending. A happier resolution the same month was the decision to supply 100 barrels of free beer to the clubs for Christmas.

The brewery workers' claim would not go away. Some clubs tried to become involved. The Crumlin Workmen's Club wrote asking for details of employees' wages. This was refused. When the deferred pay question cropped up again in January 1920, the board responded by appointing yet another wages sub-committee 'to go into the matter'.

The immediate dispute was not resolved until February and not every worker survived the bruising experience. The minutes of 18 February 1920 concluded: 'Resolved that the

BOLD APPROACH: The United Clubs Brewery soon ensured their name was on the stonework at the Crown Brewery. Note that the brewery extension built by D.&J. Jenkins has been further extended upwards to the same height as the original brewhouse

secretary be instructed to inform Mr David Jones, the dispatch clerk at the brewery, that the directors would be glad if he would endeavour to obtain another appointment.'

Relationships with other breweries were little warmer. When the South Wales Brewers' Association surprisingly wrote inviting the company to join, the board turned the offer down flat. In fact, the clubmen were mounting a campaign attacking conventional breweries. A poster sent to clubs listed the reasons for taking its beers:

1. Can your club afford to help to pay for the losses on brewery tied houses?
2. Is there any reason why you should not take advantage of the better value offered by the Club Brewery? (Many brewers charge our clubs 5s or 6s per barrel more than the Club Brewery prices.)
3. Does your committee pay this higher price for any of your supplies?
4. Can we convince you that our products are quite as good? (Our beers are brewed from pure malt and hops – no chemicals.)

The poster concluded with an appeal. 'Most clubmen combine in trade unions and co-operative societies to protect their own interests. Why not support your own brewery exclusively, and take advantage of combined trading?' At the bottom was a series of snappy slogans. 'Try it – Buy it – And don't be talked out of it. Spend where you save.' The company was also widening its appeal. 'Bonus on purchases to all clubs, whether shareholders or not.'

Trade was slowly picking up. The brewery found it necessary to invest in bigger casks, swapping kils (18 gallon casks) for much larger hogsheads (54 gallons) in a two-for-one exchange deal with Hicks Brewery of St Austell, Cornwall. More were bought from even further afield from George Younger of Alloa in Scotland.

Loans were also beginning to be made to clubs. Ynysddu Workmen's received £100 in April. These helped guarantee business, but they were of no avail if the beer was not up to scratch. Complaints about the quality continued to circulate, so that the full board called a meeting with the brewer at Pontyclun in March. 'The brewer was questioned particularly as to the gravity of the beer. The brewer then left and after further discussion Mr George Davies proposed, seconded by Mr J.P. Davies, that as from 1st April the brewer be instructed to increase the gravity by one degree (to 1040).'

The board members were quite enjoying their new authority. 'Resolved that a deputation should visit distillers for the purpose of obtaining supplies.' All expenses were paid for the three-man trip to Scotland, plus an allowance of 30s a day. On 2 July the members of the national executive of the CIU visited the brewery and were lavishly entertained from the time they arrived in Cardiff. But the directors were still splashing around in unfamiliar waters. In the summer the simmering wages wrangle heated up again. The board had been considering offering 5s a week over the standard rate, but during negotiations the workers had walked out, angering the directors.

At a board meeting on 28 July, the secretary reported that 'the men did not recommence work until 10.30 this morning'. The directors were in a bitter mood and withdrew their increased offer. They went further: 'Resolved that the lost time should be worked back by the employees' and 'Resolved that notice should be given to the employees on Friday'.

A crippling confrontation was only avoided by the action of Syd Hall, the district organizer of the Workers' Union, who attended a meeting of directors on 4 August and submitted the terms agreed between the South Wales Brewers Association and brewery employees elsewhere. 'After hearing Mr Hall, it was resolved that such terms should apply to the employees at the brewery.' The notices given to the workers were withdrawn.

It had been a traumatic first year for all concerned. In the end the brewery had produced 9,780 barrels. This was probably only half of what had been hoped. When the head brewer, Mr W.J. Rogers, had been appointed, he had been granted a commission of 3d on every barrel produced over 20,800 a year. But the unique venture had survived in a hostile world. Not only did other breweries resent the new competition, but the political leaders were opposed to the trade. Prime Minister Lloyd George favoured prohibition while the Welsh national party campaigned on an anti-alcohol platform. Many other breweries at the time were struggling. In October 1920 the clubmen had been offered the chance to buy the Cefn Viaduct Brewery near Merthyr Tydfil, but after inspecting the premises had decided not to proceed. The company also pulled out of another expensive venture when it did not go ahead with its building plans in Mill Street, Pontypridd, instead deciding to sell the site.

Chairman Huw Richards, speaking at the first AGM at the New Park Liberal Club in Cardiff on 23 October 1920, told the seventy-five delegates present: 'The directors have pleasure in congratulating the company upon the very successful initial year's working.' A profit of £2,265 had been made. 'The loyalty of the individual shareholders, and

South Wales & Monmouthshire United Clubs Brewery Company, Limited.

CAPITAL — — £50,000.

Directors.

Representing Individual Shareholders.

H. T. RICHARDS, Pontypridd, Chairman. DAN JAMES, Ynyshir.
G. DAVIES, Blackwood. D. JONES, Ferndale.

Representing Clubs.

J. P. DAVIES, Ferndale. H. HOWE, Risca.
J. T. JONES, Blaenclydach. D. J. SMITH, Newbridge.

Co-opted Directors Representing Executive Committee of the South Wales Branch of the Club and Institute Union.

A. PEARCE, Porth. G. PHILLIPS, Aberavon.

Secretary:—J. W. KINSMAN, F.C.A.

Solicitor. **Auditor.**
E. T. DAVIES, Pontypridd. H. E. SWEETING, F.C.A., Chartered Accountant, Cardiff.

Bankers.
LONDON JOINT CITY & MIDLAND BANK, LTD.

REGISTERED OFFICE: 2 & 3, TAFF STREET, PONTYPRIDD.

REPORT.

THE Directors beg to submit the Annual Report and Balance Sheet for the year ended 30th June, 1920.

The authorised Share Capital of the Company at the date of the Accounts, 30th June, 1920, was £25,000. This, since that date, has been increased to £50,000 by the authorisation of 25,000 Ordinary Shares of £1 each.

The issued Share Capital at the date of the Accounts amounted to £25,000, made up of 10,000 7% Preference Shares of £1 each, and 15,000 Ordinary Shares of £1 each.

	£ s. d.	£ s. d.
The Profits on Trading and Profit and Loss Accounts for the year, after charging Management Expenses and providing for Excess Profits Duty, amount to	...	4796 9 5½
Out of this has been provided Depreciation	1384 0 0	
Sinking Fund	1146 10 0	2530 10 0
Leaving	...	2265 19 5½
Out of this the Directors recommend the payment of the 7% Dividend on the Preference Shares, which will absorb	490 0 0	
And a 10% Dividend (less tax) on the Ordinary Shares, which will absorb	1050 0 0	1540 0 0
Leaving a balance to be carried forward to the credit of next year's account of	...	£725 19 5½

LOYALTY PAYS: *The first annual report showed a trading profit of £4,796*

STUTTERING START: The Federation Brewery of Newcastle raised funds by touring the pit villages with a horse-drawn cart, after losing £8,000 on a bad brewery at Alnwick which never produced a drop. Their first brew was not until 1921

particularly of the clubs and club shareholders has been particularly gratifying, and there is no doubt that today this company stands pre-eminent in the country as the most important club union brewery.'

This was no idle boast since the mighty Northern Clubs Federation Brewery of Newcastle, which had also been founded in 1919, had stuttered at the start. Its first brewery in Alnwick had proved unsuitable, and it was not until it bought Graham's Brewery in Newcastle in 1921 that the northern giant took off.

'The new venture has been supported well by the clubs interested, and this support has indicated to the directors the need for a considerable development and extension of the company's plant and buildings. Various plans and schemes for increasing the output are well in hand, and it is hoped that before another twelve months have elapsed, the position of the company will be infinitely better than it is today.'

The work in hand included the installation of six new fermenting vessels, but the expansion was premature. The next year demand increased only marginally, as trade was badly hit by a coal strike. In 1921 10,072 barrels were produced (weekly average 193, compared to 188 in 1920). There were also plans for a bottling hall, but this project was repeatedly put off because of lack of funds and not carried out until 1930. Bottling of popular brands like Bass and Guinness was meanwhile carried out for the clubs brewery by the Rhondda Valley Brewery of Pontypridd.

The board's lack of expertise was still exposed by transport problems, even though two more lorries had been bought. Casks regularly went missing on the Great Western Railway. Clubs in Monmouthshire complained of delayed deliveries, and eventually decided to set up their own brewery, the Gwent Union Clubs Brewery, in an existing brewery at Fleur-de-Lis near Risca.

During the immediate post-war period a number of clubs breweries were established in

STOUT ASSISTANCE: The Rhondda Valley Breweries of Pontypridd and Treherbert bottled Guinness and other beers for the clubs brewery

Britain, especially in the Midlands and North of England. In the spirit of the clubs' movement, the breweries helped each other. A delegation from the proposed West Midlands Clubs Brewery of Willenhall, near Wolverhampton, visited the Pontyclun brewery in September 1920 and in the autumn of 1921 a Clubs Breweries Federation was formed at a meeting in London.

The Pontyclun company could have bought the Fleur-de-Lis plant and premises itself, but was happy to let the Monmouthshire clubs strike out on their own, and even actively assist them, as was shown by the minutes of 16 March 1921: 'The question of the purchase of the Fleur-de-Lis Brewery, which is now for sale, was discussed. It was finally resolved that if the Monmouthshire clubs wished to purchase it for themselves, this company would lend money to them on the security of their shares in this company.'

At least two directors, including the chairman Huw Richards, attended the meeting of the Monmouthshire clubs buying the brewery, and some were involved in both companies. One of the Pontyclun directors, George Davies of Blackwood, became secretary of the new venture and the account of the new Gwent Union Clubs Brewery was guaranteed to the amount of £2,900 by the company. The Pontyclun brewery also sold Fleur-de-Lis various vessels. The spirit of co-operation did not mean there was no friction. For instance there was the case of the missing pipe which caused much correspondence. The minutes of 15 March 1922 record:

'A discussion ensued on the reported shortage of ten feet of piping in the old round [circular fermenting vessel] purchased by the Gwent brewery and on their request for compensation. It was finally resolved that the company refuse to accept any responsibility.'

After more correspondence, this decision was overturned on April 24. 'A letter was read from the secretary of the Gwent brewery with reference to the rounds originally purchased from this company. After lengthy discussion it was resolved that this company pay for the ten feet of copper piping which was missing.'

The cost was £3. Despite this sum, the Gwent venture was not a success. There was talk of widespread mismanagement – with one director ending up in court – and constant problems at the brewery. In 1926 Pontyclun had to supply beer to their neighbours in the Gwent brewery's own casks. In 1928 the company was appealing to the Clubs Breweries Federation for help. But no one was prepared to throw good money after bad – and that included Pontyclun.

The chairman, secretary and solicitor of the Gwent clubs brewery met their opposite numbers at Pontyclun early in July 1928. They were desperate, as the minutes of the general purposes committee revealed: 'The officials of the Gwent brewery had approached this company to explain that they were in financial difficulties, and practically unable to continue business and seeking any assistance and advice that could be given. They had to all intents and purposes placed themselves in the hands of this company, and were prepared to consider amalgamation, taking over or working arrangements on any reasonable conditions.'

George Davies (the Gwent secretary who was also a director of the United Clubs Brewery) gave 'the history of the company and of the difficulties and unfortunate happenings that had led up to its present position'. Despite brotherly sympathy, Pontyclun felt the venture was beyond salvation: 'The committee felt that it was impossible to recommend the board to give any financial assistance because, in view of the state of the Gwent brewery, there was little security that if such financial help were given, it would cure the trouble.' Above all, they had no faith in those steering the sinking ship: 'Under the present form of management there was a distinct possibility that this company would continue to lose money.'

Seven years after the brewery was launched, its affairs were wound up. A meeting of shareholders on 28 July 1928 resolved to pass over their shares to the United Clubs Brewery, and the clubs involved were again directly supplied from Pontyclun, Crown buying 200 casks from the folded firm. The failure of the Gwent clubs concern shows how well Crown did to survive the depression when many other companies collapsed.

The Glamorgan company did consider buying another troubled brewery in 1924. The secretary of the Cefn Viaduct Brewery attended a board meeting in April when he asked the directors 'to consider purchasing the shares in that company with a view to acquiring their trade and business'. Negotiations were started with the Merthyr Tydfil firm but came to nothing. The purchase could have meant a major change of direction since the Cefn company had sixty tied houses. Instead, the business was auctioned in 1925.

The United Clubs Brewery had, however, made one significant diversification. In 1922 the CIU had bought a large hall at Langland Bay near Swansea as a convalescent home for club members. From the start the brewery ran the adjoining hotel and soon began negotiations to buy the freehold from the CIU. This was not completed for around £20,000 until the 1930s. The Langland Bay Hotel, set in a delightful stretch of the Gower peninsula, was a prestige project. The home had been opened in 1922 by MP CW Bowerman accompanied by the Mayor of Swansea. In July 1924 it was visited by Ramsay MacDonald, Prime Minister of the first short-lived Labour government. But the hotel was never profitable and absorbed much of the brewery directors' time, right down to the fine detail of the design of napkins.

'Mrs Murison [the manageress] appeared before the board with a requisition for additional cutlery, crockery and silver teapots. These were approved and the questions of additional chairs and drugget [table covering] for the ballroom and repairs to the greenhouse were left to the chairman and secretary to arrange.'

Even the directors' ear for music was sought, as the board minutes of July 1927 reveal: 'Mr George Davies at the request of Mrs Murison raised the question of the efficiency of the orchestra at Langland Bay. It was decided unanimously that Mrs Murison be asked to accept responsibility herself for the orchestra, and to make such changes and arrangements as she thought advisable.'

SEASIDE HAVEN: Langland Bay on the Mumbles was the CIU's convalescent home for club members in South Wales. The clubs brewery ran the neighbouring hotel

The hotel was becoming an expensive drain on resources and in October that year it was first proposed that the company try to sell their lease or let the premises. But it was not to prove easy to escape from Langland Bay – and it took the company another thirty years to break the link.

Trade was difficult during the decade, with overall demand for beer in Britain in decline while taxation remained high, with sharp rises in beer duty in the early 1920s. But the clubs brewery was in one of the few growth areas of the market. While the number of pubs in England and Wales declined by 10 per cent to 56,112 from 1913 to 1939, the number of clubs doubled between the wars from 8,738 to 17,362. This was particularly marked in the period immediately after the formation of the brewery as, swelled by the growth of ex-servicemen's organizations, the number of clubs increased by 2,614 in the three years from 1920–1922, more than cancelling out the closure of 1,984 pubs. The growth of clubs in South Wales was especially strong. From little over 100 registered clubs in Glamorgan and Monmouthshire in 1896, the number had expanded to 258 by 1918 and more than doubled again to 534 by 1930. In Cardiff alone the number of CIU affiliated clubs grew from thirty-one in 1921 to sixty ten years later.

At the Glamorgan Quarter Sessions in January 1923, JP Ben Davies claimed that for every licensed house closing there was a club or two opening not far away. He blamed Sunday closing in Wales and believed it was 'manifestly unfair' that clubs could throw open their doors on Sunday while pubs had to shut. The report of the Royal Commission on Licensing in 1931 said the club had become 'a formidable competitor to licensed premises'. If the Crown Brewery could corner a substantial share of this growing market, it could not fail to shine.

One of the brewery's ploys in cementing the close relationship between the company and its club customers was a succession of brewery visits by parties of committee officials. These boisterous occasions soon got out of hand – 'It was felt there had been some abuse of this privilege' – and in July 1923 the board laid down rules restricting numbers (no more than twnety-five) and frequency of visits (no more than one a year). 'It was further decided that the calling at the brewery by club parties early in the morning when proceeding on an outing should be discouraged.'

In 1922 annual production rose to 11,500 barrels after the company had decided to supply non-CIU clubs and then jumped again in 1923 to 14,826, a weekly average of 285 barrels compared to 193 only two years before. A happy chairman Huw Richards told the AGM in October 1922: 'The company has every reason to congratulate itself upon the exceptionally successful year's working, particularly having regard to the fact that during the whole of the year's trading there has been a terrible slump in industry.

There is an ever-increasing demand for supplies from our company, which entirely justifies the action of the board eighteen months ago in undertaking to all intents and purposes a reconstruction of the inside of the brewery premises.' These improvements included a new mash tun, copper and hopback. 'During the year the directors have had an opportunity of conferring with the directors of other clubs breweries, and it becomes increasingly evident that this company continues as the most important club union brewery.'

The board received one sharp jolt early in 1924 when Hopkins Morris, the Independent

Liberal MP for Cardigan, drew first place in the ballot for private members' bills. He decided to introduce a Temperance (Wales) Bill which would not only have allowed areas to vote on a local veto on licensed premises, but also have treated clubs the same as pubs, ending their right to open on Sunday. Seriously alarmed, a special meeting of the board was called at New Park Liberal Club in Cardiff on 9 February 1924. 'The chairman explained that the object of calling the meeting was to consider what steps should be taken for the purpose of countering the Temperance (Wales) Bill. It was then decided that the chairman (Huw Richards), Mr George Davies, Mr J.P. Davies and the secretary be instructed to journey to London and to take such steps as they thought advisable for the purpose of opposing the Bill.'

Their lobbying paid off. On 15 February the bill was aborted at birth when it was 'talked out' in the House of Commons. The *Brewers' Journal* declared that 'the fact is the [Labour] Government were so bombarded with protests from working men's clubs and from other sources [MPs received more than 250,000 letters and postcards against the bill] that they dared not give their benediction to the measure as it stood, and there is little doubt that they felt considerable relief when the bill was shelved indefinitely.'

The supporters of prohibition were bitterly disappointed. Lloyd George, in a speech in Brighton on 4 March, reflected their anger: 'Here was an appeal from a small nation, which has been made in my memory for over thirty years, to have a right to deal with one of the most terrible social evils that can afflict its people . . . and it was flung out.'

The bill was the eighteenth local veto measure for Wales introduced into the House of Commons. Like the others it failed. More significantly the power of the temperance movement was fading, though it was not recognized as a spent force until the early 1930s. At the next general election almost all the supporters of the bill were voted out.

One of the reasons for the temperance movement's decline was that the drunk had largely staggered off the streets. Restricted opening hours introduced during the First World War had not been lifted, unemployment and prices were high and there were more alternative ways of spending spare money, like the cinema.

Even the clubs brewery could not escape the effects of the depression. After reaching a barrelage of 14,826 in 1923, production barely increased over the next decade, reaching a peak of 16,788 barrels in 1928 before falling back to 14,940 in 1933.

The capacity was there but not the trade. Delegates visiting the AGM at the Cathays Liberal Club in Cardiff in October 1924 were taken by charabancs to the brewery to see the completed improvements. The brewhouse was now claimed to be 'equipped in the most up-to-date fashion' and would 'bear comparison with any other brewery company of a similar capacity'. Electricity had finally been installed at the coal-fired plant. But there was no spark in the economy.

Chairman Huw Richards told the AGM in 1925: 'The profit shown on the year is considerably less than that of last year, and is accounted for entirely by a considerable falling off in the output. This falling off is accounted for mainly by the depression in trade in the whole of the South Wales area, and in some cases by circumstances in some of our clubs themselves.' The trade was so flat the clubs even agreed to a 2s reduction in the discount paid to them 'in order to ensure easier financial conditions for the company'. At the same time prices were held down.

The CIU in 1925 had been pressing the Chancellor of the Exchequer to reduce beer duty. 'Some relief for the beer drinker is long overdue,' claimed the *Yorkshire Post*. 'There is, indeed, a considerable volume of opinion in the country, not confined to working men's clubs, that if beer and tobacco were cheaper less would be heard of industrial unrest.' They were ominous words.

In 1926 came the General Strike. The mining valleys of South Wales felt the full force – as did the brewery which not only lost considerable trade but also had to make regular donations to local relief committees and distress funds. Strikers were even supplied with bread and cheese at the brewery, and doubtless a pint or two.

The board drew the line at handing out free beer to clubs, though when a delegation from Barry Dock Liberal Club called asking for a price reduction, the club was granted a free hogshead after their appeal was rejected. Later, clubs which had been given an advance on their Christmas beer allowance were told this had been converted into 'a strike allowance'.

In the strained times rumours spread rapidly. Director Mr E. Heycock of Taibach told the General Purposes Committee that 'Mr Griff Phillips (a former director) had been openly stating in the Aberavon Club that the gravity of the beers supplied had been reduced to 1032 – a drop of at least eight degrees'. The secretary was instructed to write to the club committee asking them 'to take measures to prevent a repetition of something which if persisted in might severely damage the company'.

Yet despite all the problems, the board remained optimistic. Chairman Huw Richards told the 1926 AGM in October that the directors were 'sanguine that when the present coal troubles are over . . . the company will make more progress within the twelve months following the end of the dispute than it has made at any time during its existence. They are led to this opinion by the loyalty which has been shown through the whole of the last six months by our clubs and by the fact that there has been established during the last year a number of new clubs whose intentions of dealing almost entirely with our company have been expressed very plainly.' In adversity stronger links were forged between the brewery and its club customers.

The company's bankers did not take the same view. At the beginning of November they objected to the payment of a dividend to shareholders out of reserve funds owing to the company's large overdraft. This resulted in the dividend being delayed, with payments eventually sent out 'district by district' as funds came in to meet them.

In the difficult conditions, commercial breweries resented the ace held by clubs in being able to open on Sunday. This trump trading card could always beat the breweries' tied houses, whose front doors were firmly closed on the Sabbath (even if some back doors were left ajar). A delegate to a meeting of the South Wales Trade Defence League in 1927 under W.H. Brain of the Cardiff brewers reflected the feeling of breweries and pub landlords alike when he said: 'In the old days people used to attend church and afterwards go straight into a public house for a glass of beer. Today they ignore the churches altogether and spend their Sundays in clubs.'

Despite their annoyance the commercial breweries could not afford to ignore the club trade. Indeed, they were not above offering a little financial inducement in order to get their beer on the bar. Brithdir Ex-servicemen's wrote in April 1927 asking the clubs brewery for

LOYALTY PAYS

an allowance for their steward and secretary based on the number of barrels sold – as was done by other breweries. Pontyclun refused to make such payments, but noted that Rhymney Brewery, Crosswells of Cardiff and Devenish of Weymouth were handing out money in this way.

In February 1929 the board decided to alter the way they repaid the loyalty of club customers. This issue had first been seriously considered in 1925, when it had been proposed that instead of sending out Christmas beer, a bonus be declared on the basis of each club's annual business with the brewery and the sum sent by cheque. The directors then had put off making this major change of policy. Now this cash not cask strategy was implemented as sales were improving again. 'After consideration of the output of the company, it was decided that the present basis of Christmas allowances be abolished, and that in future years a bonus of an agreed sum per barrel be made to clubs in substitution therefor.'

The change was welcomed by most clubs. Indeed Maesteg Catholic Club had been pressing for the new system. As the directors said in their report for 1930, when the company made a profit of £11,466 and out of this paid £3,117 in bonuses: 'The directors feel that the adoption of the system of bonus on purchase has been appreciated by club committees and this has been demonstrated by the increased call for our productions. Nearly £600 more has been distributed amongst the purchasing clubs than there was during the previous year.'

In May 1931 the bonus scheme was fine tuned with an extra 2s a barrel paid to those clubs whose business topped a fixed figure, while 100 per cent trading clubs were given an extra 3d a barrel. The bonus scheme was the system on which the substantial growth of the clubs brewery was to be built. It ensured that loyalty paid.

BEATING THE DEPRESSION

1930-1939

Despite the dire depression of the early 1930s, the United Clubs Brewery laid solid foundations in this period for the more prosperous years ahead. Following the introduction of the bonus scheme in 1929, attention turned back to the basics – the beer.

The brewhouse had been overhauled and modernized early in the 1920s, but the directors had repeatedly put off one major financial commitment – establishing their own bottling plant. It was not an issue they could avoid forever. After 1920 bottled beer had become the brightest sector of the brewing industry. Sales surged while draught beer declined. Despite the cost, Crown could not afford to be left behind. Already other club breweries had begun bottling and Pontyclun consulted both York and Medway about their operations. In December 1928 a bottling sub-committee was set up, though almost a year later the directors still had misgivings about going ahead, as is revealed by the minutes of the board meeting of November 1929: 'The general feeling was expressed that the financial position of the company did not permit an immediate start being made with the proposed scheme. It was, however, decided that the same committee be re-elected to deal with the matter of the bottling plant and that they be authorized – when they thought the time suitable – to bring forward a concrete scheme for the consideration of the board.'

Meanwhile in June 1930 the company asked Glovers of Neath to bottle national brands like Bass, Guinness and Worthington for them, and considered the possibility of a half-way house – installing plant at the brewery to chill and carbonate their own beer in cask which could then be sent to the bottlers for packaging. However, a representative of engineers Adlam & Sons of Bristol advised that this would be almost as costly as carrying out the whole process at Pontyclun.

Instead plans were drawn up for a bottling plant at the brewery, and on 18 August 1930 the sub-committee under chairman Huw Richards took the plunge and recommended that they go ahead 'forthwith'. The board at last agreed and decided to involve club members in the venture. 'As a means of advertising the establishment of this new side of the company's business, it was decided to offer all club men in South Wales two prizes of 5 guineas each for suitable names for the two bottled beers which are proposed to be put on the market.' This contest proved a success with over 800 suggestions received. The two winning entries were

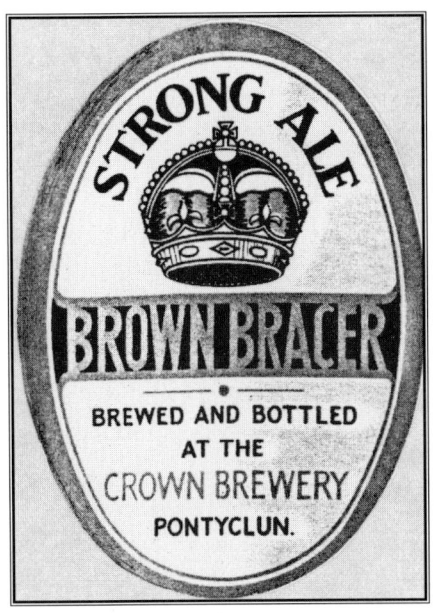
BROWN BRACER: One of Crown's first bottled beers

'Brown Bracer' for bottled XXXX from Mr T.H. Phillips of Ton Pentre and 'Crown Sparkler' for bottled CPA from Mr D.J. Jones of Blaenllechau. Secretary J.W. Kinsman tried to register these trade names, but the Trade Marks Registration Department refused to accept them.

There were other hiccups, as the company struggled with a whole host of new suppliers from manufacturers of bottles and crates to stoppers and labels. Bottling was a whole new business. The sub-committee met at the brewery on 11 December 1930 to see the new line rattle into action for the first time. They were disappointed: 'As certain pieces of plant had not been received, the installation as arranged was not fully working.' However, it was completed and in operation by Christmas.

The two beers were bottled in three sizes — half-pints (at 3s 3d a dozen); pints (6s) and two-pint flagons (11s 6d). The recommended retail prices were 4½d, 8d and 1s 3d. Within a few weeks, the cost of a dozen flagons was dropped to 10s 6d (recommended price 1s 2d), and in June 1931 the price of half-pints was reduced to 3s on the understanding that the charge to drinkers would be 4d a bottle. A dozen pints fell to 5s 6d.

There were similar adjustments in personnel. On the head brewer's suggestion, a bottling foreman had been appointed to control the new department. However, the original foreman, Mr Rowson, was replaced in March 1931 by Haydn Thomas from Buckley's Brewery of Llanelli.

The new plant helped the company beat the depression as the profit on bottled beers was higher than for draught. Chairman Huw Richards highlighted this in his annual report at the end of 1931: 'The earning capacity of the company has been considerably increased during the year under review by the installation of the equipment necessary for the bottling of our own and foreign beers.'

The new lines also made the company for the first time seriously consider marketing. Bottled beers could be sold further afield than draught beer, and many like Guinness Extra Stout and Worthington White Shield had strong brand names. Draught beers were normally just sold as bitter or mild. Previously the company had only produced a few ashtrays and waiter trays, and pipes that were given as Christmas gifts. They were reluctant to try anything more ambitious because of the cost and the general feeling that they did not need to advertise their beers since their customers bought them out of loyalty to their own brewery. The board minutes of November 1928 record: 'A representative of Messrs Raphael Tuck & Co appeared before the board with a suggestion for show cards. After considerable discussion it was decided that the company were not in a position to go to the expense of this show card themselves, but if the matter were taken up by the Club Breweries Federation they would be prepared to consider adopting it.' A few months later they opposed the setting up of a propaganda fund by the federation. They even objected to the federation's advert in the *Club Journal* magazine. Gradually, however, they began to recognize the importance of getting their name on the bar. In May 1930 the board ordered 1,000 water jugs from Prosser of Port Talbot. Two months before a large order had been placed for 1,200 waiter trays in two shapes, round and oblong.

When the bottled beers appeared, a dozen pints of the dark and light ales were sent as samples to each trading club committee, and other measures were discussed. 'Consideration was given to a tender for metal oval tablets for advertising the bottled beers.' The price proved too high for the board to swallow, but in February 1931 500 show cards featuring the bottled beers were ordered.

In addition, the company decided to employ more travellers. Previously only the former foreman, Tom Rich, had visited clubs selling the brewery's beers. As a prominent clubman who became vice-president of the South Wales branch of the CIU, he could sway the decisions of many club committees. In August 1931 Mr L.C. Jones of Newport was briefly appointed to cover Monmouthshire. Less than a year later one of the directors, Evan Rees, resigned from the board to represent the company in West Wales.

The old method of promoting club beer through brewery visits was again giving cause for concern. In October 1931 the minutes record: 'The board considered the reports of certain directors who had attended visits of club parties, some of which had not been a credit to the movement.' The board resolved to limit parties to twenty members, admission would only be by special ticket and the stay on brewery premises would be restricted to two hours. Priority was given to clubs which had not previously visited the brewery.

The move into bottling also prompted the brewery to look hard at the two beers being produced – and wonder if they should be offering a wider range? The directors started at the wrong end of the dip stick. In May 1930 the board asked customers if they would be interested in a stronger beer? The response was underwhelming. Clubs were not interested in a more expensive product. However, a cheaper, weaker brew might go down well in the hard-pressed mining valleys.

The present beers had an above-average gravity of 1040. There was scope for lower-gravity brews. After a sharp budget increase in beer duty, the directors decided in September 1931 to introduce two weaker brews with a gravity of 1034, to be known as XXX and PA, selling at £5 a barrel. The existing draught beers, XXXX and CPA, would continue to be sold at £6 per barrel with a slight increase in gravity. The new brews would be 6d beers compared to 7d a pint for XXXX and CPA. A new bottled mild beer, 'Club Brew', based on the 6d XXX was introduced, and Crown Sparkler would in future be bottled from the new PA. Brown Bracer was unchanged, except in price.

'Every avenue was explored with a view to giving the clubs the greatest possible benefit in gravity and price without hurting unduly the financial stability of the company,' said the board. However, there was a price to pay. The wastage allowance of one barrel in thirty-six was done away with and the 2s discount abolished.

Some clubs were far from happy with the new arrangements. 'A deputation attended from the Mountain Ash Hibernia Club seeking a reduction in prices and more particularly the restoration of the one in thirty-six allowance,' recorded the board minutes the following

RACKING wooden casks of CPA in the old brewery – but did the company need a wider range of draught beer?

month. The directors rejected the appeal. Many more clubs wrote to protest. Cymmer Pioneer Club even had the new beers analysed, much to the brewery's annoyance: 'The wrong impression which had been circulated by members of that committee should be countered with the least possible delay.' The chairman and secretary were authorized to visit the club and deal directly with the 'very unsatisfactory' situation. It was later decided to supply some clubs with the gravities of the beers. Breweries usually kept these figures a closely guarded secret.

Perhaps the simmering unrest among many clubs lay behind the decision in November 1931 to increase the club bonus from 1s a barrel to 1s 6d. The extra rate for 100 per cent trading clubs was doubled from 3d to 6d.

The clubs might have been even more upset if they had known of another development. The board had decided to step over the threshold into the pub bar. In July 1930 a move to secure a tie on the Farmers Arms at Glyncorrwg was narrowly defeated by six votes to five. But the issue would not go away. The next month E. Haycock of Taibach – a director representing clubs – gave notice that 'at the next meeting he would raise a discussion upon the policy to be adopted in future by the board in connection with endeavouring to obtain the benefit of the trade in licensed houses, either by purchasing, renting or tieing'. Surprisingly the question did not kick up a storm of protest when discussed in September. 'Mr Heycock moved, it was duly seconded and unanimously agreed to that in future the board should consider on its merits any application or suggestion for the purchase, renting or tieing of any licensed property.'

Perhaps opponents of the policy aimed to stifle any development of a tied estate by objecting to the merits of each pub. Details about the sale of the Colliers Arms at Blackwells were 'allowed to lie on the table'. More likely, the directors were prepared to consider any options to gain more business in a deeply depressed market.

Certainly club stewards knew all about squeezing the last drop of beer out of every barrel, as a celebrated court case illustrated. The *South Wales Echo* reported on 17 November 1931, under the headlines 'Seven more pints to the barrel' and 'How some clubs make more profits': 'According to a case at Abertillery County Court today, some club stewards have to be responsible for selling more beer than they receive in the barrels.

'Albert George Rogers of the Cwm Working Men's Club sued the committee for £9 0s 2d which he alleged was due to him. Mr Rogers said that he had made an agreement that he should account for 1¼ per cent of beer in excess of that provided in the barrel which meant that he had to produce 295 pints from a barrel which contained only 288 pints.

'Mr Jenkins for the defence said that glasses were never filled to the brim in clubs, as the measures were unlike measures used in public houses which had to be imperial measures, hence the agreement under which the steward had to produce more beer than he received.

'Mr Dolman, representing Rogers, said: "It cannot be done other than by giving short measure or adding water."

'George Davies of Blackwood, secretary of the Clubs Union in Monmouthshire (and a director of the United Clubs Brewery) said that in over sixty clubs this agreement was carried out without defrauding anyone. The steward should always show a surplus of beer.

'The judge found for the defendants after a lengthy hearing, remarking that Rogers had entered into the agreement.'

The early thirties were hard years for everyone. The largest brewers in Wales, Hancocks of Cardiff and Swansea, were unable to pay a dividend for six years from 1931 to 1936. In contrast, shareholders in the clubs brewery were smiling, as dividends and bonuses were maintained. It was not done without difficulty. Huw Richards spelled out the problems at the 1932 AGM: 'The result of the year's trading has not been nearly as satisfactory as that of the preceding few years. This has been due undoubtedly to the falling off in the consumption of our products caused first by the general industrial depression, which has left less money in the hands of our clubmen for spending and, secondly, as a result of the terribly damaging effect on our business, in common with that of all other brewers, of the increased taxation on beer which was levied by the Chancellor of the Exchequer. This iniquitous tax has made things very difficult for your directors during the past twelve months, and they feel very satisfied that under such conditions they have been able to produce accounts showing a profit on the year's working.' The profit after tax was £5,767 compared to £9,767 in 1931.

> **SEVEN MORE PINTS TO THE BARREL.**
>
> **How Some Clubs Make More Profits.**
>
> According to a case at Abertillery County-court to-day some club stewards have to be responsible for selling more beer than they receive in the barrels.
>
> Albert George Rogers, of the Cwm Working-men's Club, sued the committee for £9 0s. 2d., which he alleged was due to him. Mr. A. H. Dolman represented Rogers, and Mr. G. Roy Jenkins represented the committee.
>
> Rogers said that he had made an agreement that he should account for 1¼ per cent. of beer in excess of that provided in the barrel which meant that he had to "produce" 295 pints from a barrel which contained only 288 pints.
>
> Mr. Jenkins, for the defence, said that glasses were never filled to the brim in clubs, as the measures were unlike measures used in public-houses, which had to be imperial measures, hence the agreement under which the steward had to "produce" more beer than he received.
>
> Mr. Dolman: It cannot be done other than by giving short measure or adding water.
>
> George Davies, of Blackwood, secretary of the Clubs Union, said that in over 60 clubs this agreement was carried out without defrauding anyone. The steward should always show a surplus of beer.
>
> The Judge found for the defendants after a lengthy hearing, remarking that Rogers had entered into the agreement.

STRANGE CASE: A cutting from the South Wales Echo *of 17 November 1931, about the odd practice in club cellars*

During 1932 two of the directors took part in a deputation of clubs breweries to the House of Commons to lobby MPs for a reduction in duty. The CIU also organized club demonstrations in South Wales which the brewery helped to finance. The Brewers Society, representing commercial breweries, also applied considerable pressure. But the biggest influence was the sharp drop in revenue from beer. The Government relented and in 1933 reduced duty, much to the relief of the clubs brewery. Huw Richards told the 1933 AGM: 'The removal of the 1d per pint had a wonderful effect on the company's trade, and we have been able in the last five months to recover all the ground lost in the previous seven months, and our output for the year shows a slight increase on that of the preceding year.' So pleased were the directors that the bonus was increased by 6d a barrel.

Despite pressure from the CIU and particularly the Upper Rhondda panel of the South Wales branch, the brewery came out firmly in July 1933 against declaring the gravities of its beers to the public. The *Club Journal* in August even published the gravities of 5d, 6d, 7d and 8d beers produced by twenty breweries under the heading 'Brewers' Secrets Revealed', but the clubs brewery did not approve of this move to give customers details about the beers they bought. The directors feared that this information would be used by the major brewers to capture the club trade and wipe out the clubs breweries. They resolved that the CIU be asked to 'reconsider their attitude on this matter before irreparable financial damage to clubs and clubmen is risked'. With their new lower-gravity beers, Crown was no longer sure it held the high ground when it came to beer strength.

During this difficult period the Langland Bay Hotel continued to absorb the directors' time. Even the purchase was still dragging on, with the brewery not completing the purchase of the freehold from the CIU until July 1937. Everything still had to be examined in fine detail, as the minutes of September 1933 record: 'Mrs Murison (the manageress) raised the difficulties that existed with regard to lavatory accommodation. The chairman and some of the directors explained results of their observations and it was unanimously decided to make certain alterations and extensions.'

Life was not all hard work for the directors. The meeting at Pontyclun on 1 November 1933 ended with the note: 'The board thereupon adjourned to London in order to pay visits to Messrs George Clark & Son, sugar merchants, Messrs Watney, Combe, Reid & Co, the Wine and Spirit Exhibition and the Commercial Motor Show.'

Slowly the economy was changing. From a desperate search for customers and the need to keep running costs tight, the clubs brewery found its sales graph climbing up the wall. From 14,940 barrels in 1933, annual production rose to a record 16,848 in 1934 – and kept on going, increasing by 2–3,000 barrels a year to reach 28,193 in 1938. That amounted to a weekly average of 542 barrels compared to 287 in 1933. Trade had almost doubled in five years. And that brought new problems – the desperate need for more production capacity.

As early as January 1934 the directors were discussing increasing the number of fermenting rounds. By the end of the successful year, in which the bonus reached 3s a barrel and profits after tax topped £11,000, the chairman reported that extensions had been made to the bottling department, the cellars and the garage, all paid for out of revenue. It was soon not enough.

A year later Huw Richards was declaring that 'the company's output continues to increase and every side of the company's operations shows a considerable increase upon any period in its history'. Barrellage had reached 19,883. The bonus was 4s 6d a barrel and profits were £13,838. 'It has further been decided to recognize our customers who trade with the company for bottled beers, wines and spirits by allocating a sum of 2½ per cent on turnover as a special bonus on that trade.'

In 1936 the bonus boomed to 6s a barrel on annual production of 21,498 barrels, with the extra payment to 100 per cent clubs doubling to 1s. 'During the year the great improvement in trade which exhibited itself in the accounts for the preceding year was maintained and in fact considerably improved upon.'

The brewery began to spend more on promotional items other breweries took for granted. Barrel cards were bought in April 1936 for clubs without a cellar 'supplying direct from the wood'. In November 1936 the company decided to invest in the new novelty of 'drip pads' (beer mats) for clubmen to rest their pints on: 'Resolved that 20,000 be purchased, octagonal shape, printed both sides.' The next month badges were ordered for beer pulls, followed by 10,000 dart flights in May.

In 1937 profits were £17,801 on 24,568 barrels. The bonus was 6s 6d per barrel plus 1s 6d for completely loyal customers. Huw Richards began to sound repetitive. 'The directors are very pleased once again to be able to submit a report showing a considerable improvement upon that of last year.' But behind the smiles, back-slapping and handshakes, there were a few

STRAINED RELATIONS: The South Wales brewery was often at odds with other clubs breweries like Northants & Leicester during the 1930s

furrowed brows. Early in 1937 the bottling equipment was already struggling to keep up with demand, and a larger plant was installed for £1,500 during the summer. Nearly double that was spent on new garages and bottling stores. Much more was needed. The chairman told the shareholders at the 1937 AGM: 'The output is now almost up to capacity and your directors have under consideration extensive alterations in the brewery in the way of new fermenting vessels, etc. This they hope to put in hand during the coming year.' The plan was to extend the old brewery, an idea which had first been proposed early in 1935.

By now two new men held the reins of day-to-day power at Pontyclun. In February 1936 head brewer Mr W.J. Rogers, who had been the company's first brewer in 1919, died at his home near the brewery. A military man, he was so tall a special coffin had to be built by the carpenter at the brewery and his body manoeuvred down the stairs by draymen using the ropes which normally lowered barrels into pub cellars. Mr Rogers was replaced by his assistant, Lee Marsh, who had joined the brewery in 1924 from his family brewery in Blandford Forum, Dorset.

Much more controversial, and clouded in mystery, was the departure of the secretary, Mr J.W. Kinsman, who had also been with the clubs concern since its inception. He resigned a month after Mr Rogers' death. With no warning of any dispute, the board minutes of 30 March 1936 read: 'The special investigations relating to the former secretary were then discussed and after Mr Davies [the company solicitor] explained conversations he had had with him, the letter of resignation was read and it was decided that the same be accepted.' An ex-gratia payment of £150 was made to their former secretary. The board were anxious to be rid of their long-serving official. The office staff 'were directed to make a one-day appointment with Mr Kinsman to finally clear his effects on that day'. His personal assistant Miss Phillips 'was called before the board when she was directed that under no circumstances was she to do any kind of work for Mr Kinsman either during or out of office hours'.

FERMENTING CHANGE: Head brewer Lee Marsh admires the four new fermenting vessels installed in the old brewery in 1938

Next month the board refused to see Mrs Kinsman and a letter from Mid-Rhondda WMC about the resignation was handled by the solicitor. But the issue would not go away. A chartered accountant, Mr Kinsman was also secretary of the South Wales branch of the CIU and his abrupt departure from the brewery left club officials so concerned that national officers asked for a special meeting with the board. This was held on 16 May. 'Messrs Jenks and Chapman [general secretary of the CIU] stated that the object of their visit was to ascertain whether Mr Kinsman was a fit and proper person to be union branch secretary. Mr Jenks stated that they had received certain information from the branch which Mr Kinsman had challenged. They went into some details and from the statement made by Mr Kinsman it would appear that he was a much-persecuted man and that his forced resignation was to enable some members of the board getting his job.'

Mr Chapman asked questions about contract work carried out at Mwyndy; the transfer of £59 to the branch benevolent fund from the brewery, and various petty cash cheques. In reply the board explained the steps taken which resulted in Mr Kinsman's resignation 'after which the deputation expressed themselves satisfied and grateful for the assistance the board had given them in the matter'.

Afterwards, Mr Kinsman's assistant, Trevor Williams, was appointed secretary. At the end of the year neither the departure of Mr Kinsman nor the death of Mr Rogers were mentioned by the chairman in his annual report.

For a company whose sales and profits were soaring the board appeared surprisingly uneasy. Relations with the other clubs breweries in the renamed Association of Clubs Breweries were poor, with the Pontyclun company often calling for meetings to be cancelled to save expense. They even considered pulling out altogether. There was also an atmosphere of suspicion at the brewery. In October 1937 a special meeting of the board investigated the supply of petrol, beer and spirits to directors. The staff were told to keep their mouths shut and the travellers ordered not to engage in company politics: 'Warning to be given to the lorry drivers and draymen that they must not talk about the business of the company outside the yard of the brewery. Instructions to be given to the travellers [both leading members of the CIU] that they must not canvas for proxies or take part in any way in the election of directors.'

At the end of the year Huw Richards informed the board that he wished to relinquish the chairmanship, having held the post since 1919. The directors prevailed on him to stay on with the promise of a vice-chairman being appointed. In April 1938 Mr E. Heycock was voted in as vice-chairman, but died unexpectedly three months later and a further appointment was deferred.

At the same meeting in December 1937 it was revealed that one individual had been building up a substantial stake in the expanding company. The board refused to sanction the transfer of a further 440 shares to Mr D.G. Ball of Pontypridd: 'Several members referred to the recent activities of Mr Ball in endeavouring to promote a principle opposed to the general co-operative policy of the company and feelings were expressed that it would be against the company's interest to permit Mr Ball to become the holder of more shares.'

Mr Ball, however, bounced back, sending out a circular to shareholders in protest and the board had to instruct their solicitor to 'take counsel's opinion if necessary' to resolve the issue. The company's articles of association were altered to tighten up the rules governing the transfer of shares after two extraordinary meetings of shareholders during the summer.

The company's principles were not the only thing under threat. Many clubs breweries used the club sign off playing cards as their trademark. In December 1937 the Wrexham Lager Beer Company, which had adopted this device, wrote to Pontyclun pointing out their patent rights to the sign. The club emblem had to go.

In 1938, with production reaching 28,193 barrels – and a record 7s a barrel bonus plus 2s for loyal clubs – the company could no longer delay the inevitable. Head brewer Mr Marsh had already informed the board in October 1937 that 'he was now brewing to capacity'. The brewery would have to be extended. On 5 February 1938 a special meeting of the board was convened to consider plans and estimates. The company decided to change brewery engineers, the proposals submitted by Briggs of Burton-upon-Trent being preferred to Adlams of Bristol, with whom the board had been in dispute over the installation of a cask conveyor. Lee Marsh had been to Burton and he believed Briggs' plans 'provided for better general and workable conditions in the brewery'. He was supported by consultant brewer Mr L.R. Skinner of analytical chemists Murphys of St Albans, who was appointed to supervise the work. Even at this important meeting, Langland Bay intruded. The directors first had to look at architect's drawings for a porch covering the entrance to the sun lounge at the hotel, before considering the brewery schemes.

The work during the summer meant the cancellation of all brewery visits. While the reconstruction was in progress the consultant, Mr Skinner, recommended replacing their existing fermenting vessels as well. This required a further extension. Uncertainty was added to chaos when planning permission for this was initially turned down. It was only granted on appeal to the county council. As sales were increasing on every side, all head brewer Lee Marsh's skills were needed to keep the barrels rolling through the building site. But it was worth it. Chairman Huw Richards told the 1938 AGM in December: 'The extensions to our cellarage at the brewery together with considerable improvements and additions to our bottling plant, bottled beer storage and new garages have been completed, and also the erection of a new fermenting room and four new fermenting vessels and new plant to cope with these additional vessels. These extensions have already cost the company over £13,000 which amount has been paid out of revenue. The old six fermenting vessels will shortly be replaced by new ones of the type which have already been installed in the new fermenting room. The installing of these new vessels will necessitate the building of an addition to the existing room to contain them. When these additions have been completed your brewery will have the most up-to-date and efficient plant in South Wales.'

A few weeks before, on 2 October, the directors had proudly shown the national executive of the CIU round the brewery when the leaders of the clubs movement visited South Wales. It was an amiable and far from dry occasion, as the *Club Journal* recorded: 'The union executive visited Llantrisant on Sunday and were invited to pronounce judgement on club brewery produce. After the drive through heavy rain, which ceased when they reached the brewery, they expressed no reluctance.

'The various processes whereby the goodness of the malt is extracted, boiled up with hops

EXPANDING: The old brewery with the extension built in 1938

and sugars, run into great vats to ferment with yeast, and finally cooled, barrelled and bottled as club brewery beers were explained by Mr Marsh.'

The clubs brewery had hosted a lunch for the executive in Cardiff the previous day attended by the Deputy Lord Mayor. The CIU secretary, in his speech of thanks, hoped that 'the dispersal of the war clouds, which had so recently threatened, would be followed by increasing trade and prosperity'.

With a modernized brewery and rising sales, the future looked bright for the clubs brewery. The only problem was that the war clouds were not dispersing.

Heart of the Community

The United Clubs Brewery's business rested on one firm foundation – the South Wales club trade. Despite boardroom resolutions to supply pubs, no serious move was made to deliver to the Dog and Duck. It was a business under siege. Clubs were not popular with commercial breweries or licensees. Many political and church leaders viewed them with suspicion. Magistrates and the police were highly critical about their operation. It was felt they were above and beyond the law.

This hostility hardened during the harsh years of the depression in the early 1930s. The chairman of the Croydon licensing bench said: 'The present club system is unfair to the licensed trade and a blot on the social life of the community.' Many believed clubs were little more than sordid drinking dens set up to avoid the licensing restrictions.

This was certainly true in some areas. In the St James licensing division of Westminster in London no less than fifty-two clubs were struck off the register during 1931 after being convicted of offences. The Royal Commission on Licensing in the same year declared: 'We are satisfied that substantial changes in the law as to clubs are indispensable.' A magistrate at Greenwich remarked that a great many clubs should be struck off the register, adding: 'They are nothing but unlicensed public houses, in which those who run them are simply making faces, metaphorically speaking, at the licensing justices and the police.' The criticism was not confined to London. The Chief Constable of Cardiff in February 1933, in his report to the city's brewster sessions, attacked clubs as replacing the old 'shebeens' while praising pubs for being well conducted.

The powerful brewers' lobby was eager for action. They believed their business was being whittled away as magistrates pressed to close pubs. Between 1919 and 1931 the number of pubs fell by 6,703 – but in the same period the number of clubs increased by 5,898. The *Brewers' Journal* in September 1932 declared: 'The club problem has, from the brewers' and retailers' points of view, become far more acute in the last twelve months. The sudden, fiscally produced, reduction in beer consumption in that period has meant that licensed houses feel the competition of clubs even more acutely than formerly. A grave injustice to the licensed house is that a club's permitted hours may be and frequently are later than or different from those fixed for licensed houses in the area.

'Another grievance is that legally only one year need elapse between the closing of a licensed house as redundant and its reopening as a club. Owing to certain technicalities, this period is frequently reduced, with the result that it is not unusual to witness premises continuing to sell alcohol with the late licensee as manager and the late customers as members, with the difference that no licence duty as such is paid, no compensation levied, vastly lessened rates and taxes are demanded, and there is a complete absence of police supervision.'

The CIU itself was embarrassed by the number of bogus clubs which had sprung up to blacken its reputation. In 1933 it attempted to introduce its own bill in Parliament to eliminate dubious institutions run purely for profit by establishing a proper registration authority.

In Wales the clash between club and pub was more acute because clubs were able to open on Sunday while pubs were shut. As the *Brewers' Journal* pontificated in June 1935: 'Public men in all walks of life have in recent years inveighed against 'the club evil'. But sufficient attention has not been paid to the greatest anomaly of all, which exists in relation to registered clubs and licensed houses – namely the position in Wales and Monmouthshire.'

The *Journal* believed that the 'unjust' Sunday situation had given 'an impetus to the club movement' in Wales and Monmouthshire. 'The result has been not only that a large number of new registered clubs has sprung up in this area, but that in the main those existing in 1921 have been consolidated and financially reinforced. The licensed houses in those areas have not only to suffer with humility the spectacle of seeing their customers enjoy the right to

CRAZY WARNING: The CIU was constantly warning clubs not to take illegal liberties with the licensing hours – this could close the club down, as shown in this Crazy Club cartoon from the Club Journal in 1939

consume alcohol on Sundays in the numerous clubs which now abound, but have to meet the competition of such clubs during every other day of the week. The position is almost as illogical as it wellnigh could be.'

The working men's clubs in the South Wales mining valleys obviously relied on their bar sales to provide a large part of their revenue, but most were much more than the desperate drinking dens the brewing industry liked to portray. During the dark days of the depression many helped hold their hard-pressed communities together, as is revealed in this portrait of Rhymney Workmen's in the *Club Journal* of August 1936:

'In celebrating the twenty-first anniversary of the club, the committee and members entertained the officers and committee of the Monmouthshire Branch (of the CIU) and members of the district council at a dinner arranged by Mr Tom Gell, one of the club's oldest members: 260 members were present, and each was provided with a cigar, a novelty hat and a present.

'The club is in fact twenty-seven years old. It was opened at Victoria Road in 1909 but the premises were too small for the increasing membership and a site was purchased in High Street and the present premises erected at a cost of over £4,000.

'Evening classes are held at the club, and amongst the various subjects taught are arithmetic and economics; a study circle and lectures are well supported. The club has a well-stocked library to which have been added 500 books during the last two years. Numerous examinations have been held for entrance to Ruskin College summer school and several of the club's members have been successful. Six secondary school scholarships have been provided for members' children.

'The club has a Male Voice Party and Glee Party formed from club members, and provision is made for billiards, bagatelle, dominoes, cards, air rifle and skittles. At skittles the club teams have excelled all others in the Rhymney Valley in winning the cup and shield for two years in succession. Lastly but by no means least in importance, are the Outing Club, the Clothing Club and the National Savings Club.

'The membership of the club was formerly 500, but by reason of the industrial depression it has fallen to 200, so many of its members having left the district. A large proportion of the present members are unemployed – and they therefore appreciate the efforts of the club to make their burden more tolerable.'

The following year the *Club Journal*, the official organ of the CIU, showed the extent of the clubs' activities. In September 1937 the

THE SIGN of much more than just a drink

magazine noted that Blaenllechau Radical Club took ninety-three adults and eighty-three children by special train to the seaside resort of Porthcawl on their annual outing on 24 July. Caerphilly Social managed 200 adults and 300 children to Barry Island on 27 July, followed by a boat trip to Ilfracombe for a thousand adults on 3 August in conjunction with the neighbouring Llanbradach Social Club. Penygraig Labour Club outdid them all: Twenty double-deck coaches and eight saloons were required to convey the biggest party ever from Rhondda Valley to Porthcawl for the club's outing last month. There were 1,700 persons of whom 566 were children and 402 mothers. Each child was given a shilling. In arranging the outing the organizers undertook the task of conveying over 200 persons who had no connection with the club but who were anxious to join the party. To meet the enormous cost of the outing, a committee, with Mr Jack Landeg as secretary, has worked throughout the year on a variety of events including concerts. Many of the party were children and wives of unemployed members who, but for the club's efforts, would not have had an opportunity of visiting the seaside.'

Clubs were at the heart of their communities – and the movement was spreading out beyond the mining valleys and cities. The *Club Journal* of October 1938 recorded the success of one club on the quiet coast of the Vale of Glamorgan:

'Mr J.P. Davies [President of the South Wales Branch of the CIU and a director of the clubs brewery] formally opened Llantwit Major Social Club's new premises on September 16. He congratulated the club upon the acquirement of a splendid new club house, and mentioned that it was only some four years ago that the club was formed in a small building with forty members. A substantial portion of the work in connection with the new club house was carried out by clubmen volunteers who worked during weekends.'

Two years before, early in 1936, the clubs brewery had helped establish a much more distant club, the Fishguard and Goodwick Railwaymen's CIU at Brodog Hall, Fishguard, in the far south-west of Wales. The prominent public commentator Beverley Nichols weighed into the 'low subject' of South Wales clubs early in 1938, making a number of points in an article in the *Sunday Chronicle,* including: 'They have huge memberships. Some of the members simply join to get a drink,' and 'On any Sunday you can see men standing outside these clubs for the sole purpose of introducing any person who wants a drink.' He concluded: 'I could say a great deal more on the same lines, but I have said enough to prove that however estimable the aims of the original framers of the Welsh Sunday Closing Act, its net result has been to create a series of ridiculous anomalies.'

George Davies, the secretary of the Monmouthshire Branch of the CIU and a director of the clubs brewery, replied in an open letter:

'I doubt if you ever spent a Sunday in Wales, and therefore dismiss your remark that men stand outside clubs on Sundays for the sole purpose of introducing any person who wants a drink, as either the imagination of your brilliant mind or as unreliable information gathered from your temperance friends.

'The Club and Institute Union which I represent as an official in Monmouthshire is an organization of 2,767 clubs. It was established seventy-five years ago and looks after the interests of these clubs and their members.

'It owns four convalescent homes in Grange-over-Sands, Saltburn, Pegwell Bay, Kent, and Langland Bay, Swansea. The total value of these properties and their equipment is over

LOYALTY PAYS

LIVELY NIGHT OUT: The busy club on Saturday night

Heart of the Community

£90,000. The cost of running these four convalescent homes amounts to nearly £20,000 a year. This is provided by subscriptions and donations from the clubs. Other small efforts of this Union are indicated by expenditure each year of £2,500 on education and £3,000 on promoting recreation. Some brains as well as beer represented here.

'Your attack is particularly uncharitable as you were recently in the Rhondda Valley, collating information for a Page Two article in the *Sunday Chronicle* on successive Sundays, and whilst there you were hospitably received by the Penygraig Labour Club which you subsequently described as a 'Gaunt building in a narrow street'. Nothing of the kind. Whilst the Rhondda is narrow, the Penygraig Labour Club possesses very fine and substantial premises which are a credit to its pioneers; is well managed and has recently been redecorated throughout. To this I can personally testify, as I have visited it monthly for eighteen years in a professional capacity.

'Obviously when you were obtaining your information in a particular room of this club, you were too intent on the purpose of your visit to notice a photograph hung on the wall of about twenty big buses which took 700 to 800 wives and children of members for a day's outing to the seaside last summer at the club's expense.'

The clubs brewery might concentrate their attention on the cellar and bar. But for most members the club was much more than just a pipe and a pint. It was often the social centre of their lives.

BATTLE STATIONS

1939–1945

The year began quietly enough. The dust settled in the brewery as the extensions were completed by May. Club visits started again. A new bottle washing machine was bought as it was reluctantly felt that young hands should no longer be doing the work 'owing to the restrictions of the Factory Act with reference to the employment of boys'. Dungarees were ordered for the workers. The stewards' annual outing to Ascot and the employees' trip to Weston-super-Mare were arranged. Permission was given to the manageress of the Langland Bay Hotel to buy a new wireless and seek a fresh ice cream supplier. It appeared to be business as usual.

Even the battle with Pontypridd shareholder Mr Ball appeared to be over. He had refused to stand as a director at the 1938 AGM despite being nominated, instead backing one of the board. In return the contentious transfer of extra shares to him was approved.

The only scare was another Clubs Registration Bill. A nine-man deputation representing the brewery and the two local branches of the CIU rushed to London in March 1939 to lobby the House of Commons, the company footing the £200 bill for the three-day stay. Such worries were soon to appear trivial.

The reality of the imminent conflict first intruded in May. Under the heading 'Military Authorities' in the board minutes, the secretary reported that 'billeting officials had visited the brewery and earmarked the company's garages'. The directors asked the solicitor to make inquiries to see 'if there was any likelihood of any interference with the company's business'. The police assured them there would be no problems except 'in case of war'.

Hitler invaded Poland and the problems began. A special board meeting was called on 4 September, the day after war with Germany was declared. Suddenly there were a thousand new factors to consider. The bank rate had gone up and the company had to register under War Risks Insurance. A letter had been received about group arrangements for lorries. Brewing restrictions were expected. Worried about supplies, clubs were pouring in orders for beer and spirits 'in excess of the usual'. When men were called up, it was resolved that their jobs be kept open for them. Meanwhile the board decided to employ boys again.

The Langland Bay Hotel was already well prepared. 'Dan James reported on behalf of the manageress that a shelter for the employees had been provided in the beer cellar and had been sand-bagged'. The blacked-out hotel would stay open for business until the end of the month, despite reduced business.

Meanwhile at the brewery 'it was resolved that the board room should be used as an air warden's post if required and that the question of trenches be left to the brewer'. Staff were to be trained in air-raid precautions. The depth of the emergency was underlined by the final decision: 'The remaining three visits for club committees to the brewery be cancelled.'

Some customers were more heavily affected. At the next board meeting on 25 September, George Davies reported on his visit to Bedwas Workmen's Club: 'He found that all the accommodation with the exception of the bar had been taken over by the military authorities and that owing to this there had been no official opening of the new extensions.'

By now the brewery was finding it hard to get supplies. 'Mr Marsh the brewer attended and explained that certain increases in the price of materials had taken place and that he was experiencing difficulty in delivery.' Despite this, 'the board resolved that the normal number of brews should be entered weekly'.

Petrol was rationed and the secretary appealed to the authorities for a supplementary allowance, being granted a further 100 gallons a week for the lorries. Expecting to lose some drays, an extra vehicle, a second-hand Austin three-tonner, was bought for £340. This was soon followed by the purchase of a new Bedford lorry.

On 28 September, only three days after the board meeting, a special session was held to consider the Chancellor's increase of beer duty, amounting to a penny on a pint. 'It was resolved that the brewer should carry on as at present and that there should be no change in the gravities of the beers.' The prices of XXX and PA would be £5 a barrel; XXXX and CPA £6 from 2 October. Bottled beer prices were also increased.

The early 'phoney war', with no immediate fighting in the west, caused the directors to dither. The board decided that 'in view of the present crisis' there should be no election of directors at the AGM. Then after pressure from the clubs they gave way. Christmas gifts to clubs were suspended – but then reinstated in December, the board deciding to buy pipes.

Meanwhile life went on at Langland Bay. Applications were made to hold dances and it was agreed to go ahead with a new gents lavatory. Tournaments for darts, bagatelle and table skittles were held to raise money for the *Daily Mirror* Dart Board Fund.

AT THE READY: The company's fleet of seven dray lorries at the start of the war. More were quickly bought, as the brewery expected to lose their best vehicles to the war effort

In November two employees went for military training and by the end of the year there had been major changes on the board. Huw Richards stood down as chairman after twenty years following the AGM at Pontyclun Social Club on 9 December. He was later presented with a silver salver. Dan James became the new chairman and Tom Jones vice-chairman. The traveller Tom Rich was elected to the board, resigning his job to take his place at the top table.

As there were no guns firing in Western Europe, the board and employees returned to an old battleground. The workers asked for a wage increase because of the higher cost of living. On 29 January the directors refused to meet their demands in full. The following day the draymen refused to take the lorries out. Only after the union area secretary had mediated was the dispute resolved. According to the board minutes the union official 'was definitely of the opinion the men were out of order'.

There was also the climax of a major court battle over the case of the Trebanog Workingmen's Club which had been convicted of selling liquor without a licence at Porth Magistrates Court in March 1938. If this verdict had been upheld it would have affected hundreds of clubs, but on appeal to the High Court on 17 January 1940 the decision was overturned. The CIU and the brewery breathed again.

The war seemed so distant – despite the dribble of men joining up – that in February the board decided to 'make arrangements for the celebration of the twenty-first anniversary of

CALM BEFORE THE STORM: The board and officials line up for a photograph for the booklet celebrating the first twenty-one years of the company in 1940: STANDING (left to right) W. Morgan, E.T. Davies (solicitor), H.J. Pearce, Bertie Rowe, Tom Rich, H. Vaughan, E. Walton and W. Griffiths. SEATED (left to right) W. Jones, T. Jones, Trevor Williams (secretary), Dan James (chairman), Lee Marsh (head brewer), J.P. Davies and E.O. Williams

COVER of the souvenir booklet issued to celebrate the first twenty-one years

the company'. A sub-committee was appointed to arrange a party for July. But within a few weeks of the decision there suddenly seemed a lot less to celebrate.

The first jolt was just about bearable. The Chancellor raised the duty on beer again at the end of April. A special meeting of the board resolved that the extra tax had to be passed on. Clubs were informed that 'although the Chancellor had imposed a duty of 24 shillings per barrel in September and another 24 shillings this week, the gravity of the beer had not been interfered with'. The company also pointed out it had not passed on the increased cost of raw materials and rising wages. Bottled beer went up to 6s 6d a dozen for pints of the weaker Club Brew and Crown Sparkler and 7s 6d for the stronger Brown Bracer and Club Special.

The second blow was devastating. The phoney war was over. In May Hitler's army began to power its way through Holland and Belgium into France. In June the British Expeditionary Force scrambled away at Dunkirk leaving most of its equipment behind. France surrendered and Britain was left alone to face the might of an all-conquering army across the Channel.

The clubs brewery had been preparing a blitz of its own – sending deputations of two directors to clubs who were behind with their accounts. The attack on slow payers was cancelled as the grim news spread from the continent. Instead of concentrating on the anniversary celebrations, the board established a hardship committee to help the families of employees joining the armed forces. A grant was made to the local home guard. Ten guineas was given to the Spitfire Fund.

Battle Stations

Though Winston Churchill, now Prime Minister, had promised only blood, toil, tears and sweat, not everyone was pulling in the same direction. On 24 June the secretary reported that the drivers had refused to accept one of the boys from the bottling stores as a lorry mate. The board took a hard line and insisted that the boy be accepted in the interests of the war effort. But when the RAF commandeered one of the company's lorries the secretary was instructed to write to their MP about 'the exact power of the authorities and whether there was any chance to appeal'.

A muted anniversary celebration went ahead at Langland Bay Hotel on 13 July with a lunch attended by 300 delegates. There was a souvenir booklet and special pint glasses, but there was little to smile about. Everyone's mind was on the war. The toasts were for the King and the Armed Forces, then the company. Military call-ups had even reached board level, with one of the directors, Bertie Rowe, going off to join his unit.

Swansea was now a major target for Hitler's air force. That meant the Langland Bay Hotel was also in the front line. On 29 July chairman Dan James reported that the bus service to the hotel 'which had been running on certain days had stopped owing to air-raids'. The Top Cafe at the hotel was requisitioned by the military.

The bombs were dropping closer to Pontyclun and on 23 September brewer Lee Marsh asked 'that consideration should be given to an air-raid shelter for the employees'. The directors agreed one should be erected though, ever practical, they later decided that half of the space should be used as a sugar store.

Enemy aircraft were everywhere. They even destroyed the company's Christmas gifts. The secretary reported on 28 October that 'he had placed an order for ten gross of pipes but unfortunately the factory had been bombed'. Propelling pencils had to be ordered instead.

Yet at the end of the year, the annual accounts were 'exceedingly satisfactory'. The figures were so good that the company was able to declare a record bonus of 8s a barrel plus an extra half-crown for clubs trading 100 per cent with the brewery.

There might be a war on and prices had shot up, but people more than ever needed their glass or two of comfort. The CIU were even warning members against the growing practice of using clubs as improvised, late-night, air-raid shelters: 'Air-raids do not excuse drinking after time.' Such foolishness would 'be inviting another kind of raid – by the police'.

The customers were enjoying their last pints of pre-war beer. On 4 February 1941 a special meeting of the board heard that owing to restrictions on malt and hops and other brewing materials, the strength of the beer would have to be reduced. The gravities of all beers were dropped by three degrees. The question of rationing supplies was in the air and the board resolved not to open any new accounts. Pressure was also mounting in the brewhouse as the deputy brewer, Peter Clark, had been called up. In April Mr Watson of Cheltenham was appointed as temporary under brewer.

Distributing the beer was becoming a problem. The secretary reported at the end of April that 'owing to increased output during the holiday he found it necessary, due to shortage of petrol, to ask certain clubs to send lorries to the brewery for their beer'. By now nine boys were employed by the company.

Meanwhile at the Langland Bay Hotel they were counting the cost of entertaining their own soldiers. The chairman reported that 'the cafe had been evacuated by the troops and that Mr Saunders the valuer had been called in to assess the damage done'.

Loyalty Pays

From 1 June the amount of hops used had to be reduced by 20 per cent. This not only meant the ale was less bitter, but also lowered its keeping qualities. The problem of returned beer began to mount – but soon disappeared owing to another development. Rationing was introduced from 10 June after the brewer informed the board that he no longer had sufficient materials to meet all demands. It was decided to make a cut of 10 per cent in supplies of draught and bottled beers to completely loyal trading clubs and a cut of 25 per cent to other customers, based on their orders for the previous three months.

The decision was greeted by a flood of letters. Clubs which traded completely with the brewery wanted to know if they would lose their loyalty bonus if they sought supplies elsewhere. This possibility alarmed the board. The head brewer came to the rescue by finding an extra supply of malt, and it was decided to meet the demands of the 100 per cent clubs in full. All clubs would receive an extra quota for the week before the August bank holiday, and a sub-committee was appointed to deal with the allocation of any surplus beer.

The question of who received what soon generated tremendous heat. The secretary reported on 26 July that 'the secretary of Hopkinstown Non-Political had rung up at 10.30pm (while the company secretary was on duty fire-watching) and in consequence of the language used he had rung off during the conversation'.

The delicate issue of supplies was not helped when part of the brewery's hop stock – held by merchants outside Pontyclun – was destroyed by enemy action. A sum of over £1,500 was paid out under the War Risks Insurance policy.

Yet despite all these problems and restrictions, the accounts at the end of the year were again considered 'exceedingly satisfactory'. Another healthy bonus was declared. The gross profit for 1941 had been £58,227 on turnover of £322,685. This compared well with a gross profit of £39,146 the previous year. At the AGM at the Langland Bay Hotel on 13 December the delegates were treated to lunch with three free pints and a box of Whiffs. The company was in a sound enough state in February 1942 to make a substantial donation of £2,500 to Llantrisant's Warship Week.

If rationing had been a problem in 1941, it became a more desperate issue in 1942. This time Mr Marsh could not conjure up any additional malt. Production had to be cut by a quarter in January, with preference again given to completely loyal clubs.

The number of unsatisfied customers and the lower-gravity beer was a potent brew. It caused whispers to spread. In February the chairman Dan James reported 'certain rumours received with reference to the condition of the company's beers and after discussion it was resolved that in view of the fact the company had no travellers to investigate the matter, the directors should act as travellers and that all clubs should be visited'.

Malt and hops were not the only items in short supply. Manpower was also becoming a problem as more workers went away to war. The secretary called on the local Labour Exchange where the manager agreed that the brewery 'had a very strong case in support of future applications' for staff in view of the number of brewery employees called up.

Even boys were becoming valuable. The secretary reported in March that 'two boys had left the company's employ as they had obtained better wages elsewhere'. The board resolved to increase the boys' wages. Later one likely lad was 'promoted' from the bottling stores to the brewery, much to the concern of the workers there.

BOTTLING BOYS: Boys took over the bottling lines during the war

Space was also at a premium. The regional controller of the Board of Trade visited the brewery and 'earmarked the garage and cellar over the brook for storage of foodstuffs'. A temporary timber lean-to garage had to be built next to the air-raid shelter.

After another budget increase in April, beer prices went up again – this time by 48s a barrel. Beer was becoming a luxury item, with prices driven up further by wartime inflation. But like all luxuries, such as chocolates and ladies' stockings, beer was in demand.

The bonus for the first six months of the trading year was fixed at 14s, double what it was before the war. By the end of the year it was 26s a barrel, an amount that would have been unthinkable two years before. The accounts at the end of the year were again 'very satisfactory' with business having grown despite the restrictions. The staff were congratulated on helping bring the company 'to its excellent financial position'.

The war might be turning in the Allies' favour abroad, but in Britain the grip of chronic shortages was tightening. Petrol was in dwindling supply and early in 1943 distribution zones were introduced by the Ministry of Food, which meant breweries only delivered to their local areas. The board were worried this might mean losing business and took a determined stance – which paid off. In May the minutes record 'the board's appreciation of the forcible action taken by the chairman and secretary in getting such an excellent result'. The clubs brewery had escaped zoning. The minister responsible, Lord Woolton, had replied 'that there would be no necessity to disturb the existing arrangements'. The company were, however, required to convert one of their lorries to gas operation.

The war was becoming more comfortable in some respects. New beds were ordered for the fire-watchers, and in April it was resolved that a canteen and fire-watchers' room with accommodation be built at a cost of £275. Some workers were enjoying the war a little too much. The board minutes in June recorded: 'The chairman reported that the allowance to the workmen was being abused. After consideration it was resolved that the chairman should inform Mr Marsh that the men, especially lorry drivers and their mates, should not be encouraged to remain on the brewery premises after 7.30pm. In exceptional cases he should use a certain amount of discretion, but that must not be abused.'

Perhaps they were celebrating the possibility of peace? Light was beginning to be glimpsed at the end of the terrible tunnel. Certainly some were confident of victory. As early as July 1943 brewery engineers Briggs of Burton-upon-Trent wrote to the brewery 'with reference to post-war orders'. In response a Post-War Plant Committee was established to consider extending the fermenting room. In September the employees enjoyed an outing to Porthcawl.

The steady flow of requests for donations was changing from money for munitions to cash to care for the war wounded. In September the brewery set up a Hospital Fund with an inaugural amount of 100 guineas to meet the many appeals. One sum went to Cardiff Royal Infirmary's 'blitzed wards' fund.

Money was also put aside to renovate and renew their battered fleet of vehicles after the war. A deposit was paid for seven new lorries. The future was looking brighter. The outside of the brewery was even given a new lick of paint. The annual accounts were once more 'very satisfactory'. The bonus for 1943 was fixed at the same high level as in 1942, with 26s a barrel for the final four months.

Business was almost back to normal. On 22 November the chairman reported that 'trouble had arisen in the transport section over the non-payment of wages to men absenting themselves from work on recent Saturday mornings. The men refused to commence work unless matters were adjusted on the next pay day.' A deputation was received from the drivers who refused to budge from their demand. Dan James then told them 'to clear off the brewery premises immediately'. The secretary was instructed to hire lorries. 'It was also resolved that the chairman should attend at the brewery early on the following morning in the event of the trouble spreading to the brewery section.'

That dispute died down – but there was trouble at the brewery in the bottling plant. A new bottling foreman, Mr A.E. Basson, had been appointed in August, but there were constant losses in the department. On 22 January his contract was terminated and he was placed on a week-to-week basis. A few days later one of the lorry drivers was dismissed by the secretary.

The war was witnessing a shift of power within the company. Once the brewer had ruled the day-to-day business, earning more than the secretary. Mr Rogers had certainly towered over Mr Kinsman. The secretary in the 1930s was mainly responsible for the office and administration. The brewer ruled the rest. Increasingly the new secretary Trevor Williams was taking the lead. He became responsible for the transport department. The brewer, Lee Marsh, was pushed back into the brewhouse. Even bottling seemed outside his control. He rarely attended board meetings.

On 28 January 1944 the new staff hierarchy was confirmed. After a discussion on 'the advisability of a change in the control of certain departments' the board resolved that 'the secretary have charge of all departments and all employees outside the brewery'. The brewer was only responsible 'for the brewing of beer and those under his control inside the brewery'. The secretary was to be in overall charge of those in the bottling department. Trevor Williams' salary was increased by £150 a year.

Mr Marsh was not prepared to let this matter go without a stand, and at the next board meeting in February said that 'he preferred to carry on and abide by the terms of his service agreement which provided that he should superintend and direct all workmen and other servants of the company employed in and about the brewery and bottling stores . . . with the exception of those under the control of the secretary in the office and distribution department'. The board decided to give way 'in view of Mr Marsh's attitude and the terms of the service agreement'. But it was only a temporary halt in the power shift. New service agreements were drawn up.

The war restrictions were slowly easing. In April 1944 the secretary reported that 'extra brewing materials had been released in addition to the quota allowed by the food controller and that the weekly allowance of coal had been increased. In view of this it was possible to brew extra beer to the extent of forty-five barrels per week.' In July after more malt was received, a further forty barrels a week were brewed. At Langland Bay the manageress was allowed to buy a Wilton carpet. In the summer the services of chairman Dan James and director J.P. Davies, who had both served twenty-five years on the board, were recognized by a presentation of 150 guineas each.

By the end of July the brewery was talking about the possibility of bringing supplies to existing customers up to their 'pre-war level'. However, no new accounts could yet be opened. Financially the company was in a sound position. The secretary reported in September that all loans had been liquidated. The company were now only liable as guarantors to the bank in respect of three clubs to the amount of £1,600.

Meanwhile Mr Marsh was struggling to get back into the directors' good books. Two brews had been unfit for sale, one having to be destroyed. Mr Marsh was called before the board in October and in a desperate attempt to remedy the situation he suggested that 'as much as possible of the second brew should be bottled'. This was agreed but hardly helped the brewer (or the bottled beer drinker). The chairman informed Mr Marsh that the board 'was very much concerned with these mishaps'.

Despite some dodgy brews, business was booming. In November the auditors were granted an additional 100 guineas, doubling their normal fee, 'owing to the very large turnover of the company'. The extra loyalty bonus for 100 per cent trading clubs was increased to 3s a barrel. War was not bad news for everyone.

However, the expected victory on the Continent was not coming as quickly as some had hoped – and the brewery was expected to help the troops in the front line. Mr Marsh told the board on 27 November 1944 that they had been instructed to supply 12 quarters of malt a month for brewing beer for the soldiers in Italy and a substantial amount of bottled beer for the Western Front (amounting to 165 barrels a month). The board was not enthusiastic and wrote seeking clarification, resolving to take no action until a reply was received.

The Association of Clubs Breweries tried to gain exemption from the order, arguing that the clubs breweries supplied the hard-pressed working man, and that 'these supplies to the forces would further enhance the shortages amongst work people'. The Government replied that no exception would be allowed. 'Every firm of brewers must supply their quota.'

The amount of bottled beer required from the South Wales clubs brewery was altered to forty-three barrels a month bottled at Pontyclun and sixty-five barrels to be supplied to another Welsh brewery, Andrew Buchan of Rhymney, for bottling there. Malt still had to be sent to Italy. The company conceded, with the result that supplies to customers had to be cut by a quarter in January 1945.

Deliveries were further hampered by the fact that beer was going missing from the brewery. In November 1944 the police had been called in to interview the boys in the bottling stores after four cases of half-pints of Special disappeared from stock. After the chairman and secretary had investigated 'the question of the pilferages' it was decided to post a notice in the stores that anyone caught stealing would be instantly dismissed and prosecuted. Meanwhile, the company was running into a new problem. The bottling boys were growing up. One was called up for the armed forces.

The brewery celebrated VE Day on 8 May with extra wages for the employees. But the one who was really smiling was the secretary. While brewer Lee Marsh had been reprimanded by the board for interfering with a supply of malt obtained by the directors from other clubs breweries, Trevor Williams in June received a bonus of £750 and had his salary increased from £750 to £1,000 a year 'in view of the satisfactory position of the company'.

Building Hopes

1945–1954

VJ Day was celebrated on 2 September 1945, after the surrender of Japan, with extra beer sent out and another bonus to the workforce. The flags waved and the bottles tilted as the war was finally over. But the underlying colour of the occasion was grey. Britain was exhausted after all the exertions of war. The clubs brewery was in a similar state.

Three directors reported on their visit to the bottling stores at the end of August. 'All agreed that the stores were in a filthy condition, that there was no control over the boys and that the plant required to be over-hauled.' Not surprisingly there were many customer complaints about the quality of the less than sparkling ale, and heavy losses in the department. A new bottling foreman, Mr T. Darbyshire, was appointed and new, larger machinery ordered.

If the bottling department had to be rattled into shape, the brewhouse needed much more than an overhaul. The extensions completed at the beginning of the war had already been overtaken by demand. If the company was to meet tomorrow's thirst it needed to expand quickly today. A sub-committee was already looking at the possibility of further extensions to the old brewery in September in conjunction with plant firm Briggs of Burton-upon-Trent. A consultant engineer, Mr Culverwell of Westbury on Trym, near Bristol, was called in during October and made a preliminary report.

The board wanted to move rapidly. The company was financially in a very strong state. A record bonus of 28s a barrel was declared for the final four months of 1945, with an additional loyalty bonus of 3s. There was just one problem. The Ministry of Works would not grant a licence for the work to go ahead. The war might have ended, but the wartime regulations lingered long. Even the provision of concrete steps at the Langland Bay Hotel required a building licence. The brewery garages were not released by the Ministry of Food until January 1946. Other restrictions lasted much longer. In fact, to the annoyance of brewers and drinkers alike, they got worse.

Clubs were still limited to a percentage of their pre-war trade. They were unable to increase the quantity delivered. Even altering the composition of their order required a major investigation. Only after secretary Trevor Williams had interviewed club officials was Penrhiwceiber British Legion allowed by the board in February 1946 to lower their order of eight hogsheads of XXX to four, while increasing their order of CPA by the same amount from nine hogsheads to thirteen.

Clubs were clamouring for more beer and in the spring of 1946 the company was quietly confident that a new era of peace and prosperity was dawning. The board met on 22 March to review detailed plans for the brewery extensions. The £5,000 scheme was enlarged another 11 feet as the original was 'rather cramped'. Consultant Mr Culverwell was confident that it would gain official approval. Applications for extra beer from a number of clubs were approved.

In April all the hopes were dashed. That month chairman Dan James died, his position being taken by vice-chairman William Morgan. It was an ill omen. The Ministry of Works informed the board that the issue of a building licence for the extensions was deferred 'until the situation respecting materials and labour had improved'.

Worse, because of a growing food shortage, the Government determined to restrict the use of grain for brewing. Brewers were ordered to cut the amount of beer produced by 15 per cent. The depressed board at a special meeting early in May reluctantly decided that club quotas would have to be dropped by this amount and 'owing to the reduction it was resolved that no extra beer could be given for holidays and any beer returned could not be replaced'. It was a gloomy start to the post-war era.

The mood was not helped by the acrimonious wrangling over one employee. The appointment of Mr Darbyshire to supervise the bottling hall meant that the former traveller Evan Rees, who had been acting as bottling foreman, was out of a job. A prominent member of the CIU, he was promptly nominated as a director by Maesteg Workmen's Club, much to the embarrassment of the board. They resolved the situation in November 1945 by offering Mr Rees the post of checker in and checker out. He accepted but when he asked for time off to attend meetings of the CIU National Executive, this was refused. He went anyway, attending two meetings in January 1946. The secretary reported this misdemeanour, and one director, Mr W. Griffiths, moved that the board rescind their previous decision. This motion was lost by seven votes to two and Mr Rees was warned that if he took time off again he would be suspended without pay. He went anyway. Meanwhile the South Wales branch of the CIU appealed against the decision and the board agreed to meet a deputation. The crunch came in the black month of April.

The secretary reported that Mr Evan Rees had attended the National Executive meeting at Manchester on 5 April and was 'also away the day previous.' On his return he had been suspended. The board decided to take action immediately before receiving the deputation waiting outside. Evan Rees was dismissed, the co-opted board members from the CIU being instructed 'to refrain from voting'. When the branch deputation was finally admitted, they were told of the decision. The CIU men withdrew.

For two close, brotherly organizations, it was an unfortunate dispute. And one which would soon be highlighted face to face. The brewery hosted a long-arranged meeting of the CIU National Executive in Cardiff in the summer. The issue had not gone away. The national secretary of the CIU, Mr Chapman, appealed to the directors to reconsider their decision. Ammanford Social and Merthyr Tydfil Labour were among a number of clubs which protested about the treatment of Mr Rees. They were simply informed that the board 'had good and sufficient reasons for the course they took'. Later, conflicting circulars about the controversial case were distributed round clubs by both the CIU and the brewery.

The only bright spot in April was the presentation of a canteen of cutlery to one of the workers, Sidney Berry, to mark the award he had received in the Italian campaign. Men were still returning from the conflict and some of the wartime workers had to be dismissed. Among those coming back was the assistant brewer, Peter Clark.

Meanwhile the decision of the Ministry of Works not to allow the brewery extension to go ahead began to look irrelevant, perhaps even a godsend. Mr Culverwell dropped his own bombshell which effectively blew up the plans. He said that on closer inspection he believed the old brewery, built at the start of the century, was structurally unsound, with 'serious defects'. He recommended constructing 'an entirely new building' to solve the capacity problem.

The board responded in May by increasing the number of directors on the 'extensions' sub-committee from three to five and asking Mr Culverwell to visit and inspect the crumbling brewhouse every fortnight. 'Should any defects require attention endeavours would be made to put them right, but no trouble was anticipated at the moment.' They also resolved to visit other clubs breweries at Newcastle, Leicester and York to look at their layouts. They were aiming to build a new brewery – when the men from the ministry approved. Little could they imagine it would take eight years to complete their plans.

With output restricted and a move in the market towards the better class of beer, the brewery decided in June to drop their weaker brews, XXX and PA. Within days, the Government devalued this decision. Anxious to maintain supplies, in July the Ministry of Food ordered brewers to lower the average gravity of their beers by 10 per cent. This meant more beer could be brewed from less barley. The clubs brewery also dropped their price to £11 a barrel, with a recommended selling price of 11d a pint. Secretary Trevor Williams believed 'it was possible to increase the quotas of clubs to their wartime level'. But while quantity rose, quality fell. A number of clubs complained about the wishy-washy ale. Even wartime beer would have tasted good in tightly rationed post-war Britain.

Yet the clubs beer still exerted a powerful attraction. Trevor Williams complained to the board that 'a better method should be adopted' for supplying employees with their beer allowance: 'For some time this has been very unsatisfactory, in loss of time and overcrowding of the cellar.' In August 1946 the following rules were laid down:

1. All brewery employees including cask washers, cooper, carpenter, night watchmen and bottling foreman to be allowed four pints a day, Monday to Friday; two pints Saturday and three pints Sunday for those working.

2. Barmen and coalmen delivering goods one pint each delivery but not more than two pints a day.

3. Transport section not allowed in cellar but to have the use of the room adjoining the mess room for partaking of their allowance and to make their own arrangement for distribution. The allowance to be on the same basis as the brewery employees.

These new arrangements soon staggered into predictable problems: 'Owing to the abuse made of the privilege by some of the transport employees, a notice had been put up curtailing the time these employees were allowed to remain on the company's premises.'

Some workers might be reeling, but the finances of the company were very steady. At the end of 1946 a pre-tax trading profit of £62,709 was declared. Another huge bonus was given amounting to £53,876. This was more than had been paid out in the whole of the first ten years of the scheme to 1939, which had totalled £40,687. As chairman William Morgan reported: 'Demand for the company's products continued to be well in excess of the ability to supply.'

The vacant seat left on the board by the death of Dan James was filled by Mr D.G. Ball of the Celtic Club, Pontypridd, the shareholder the directors had once tried to block buying more shares.

Another sign of changing times was that in December head brewer Lee Marsh went to an exhibition in Bristol to look at 'steel barrels'. He was not impressed. The company decided to stick with wooden casks for the present. Later, in 1950 in order to keep up with repairs to the wooden barrels a second cooper had to be employed.

Rationing was also changing. It was getting worse. Trevor Williams reported in January 1947 that the supply of whisky had been cut by between five and seven cases a month. Coal, a vital fuel in the brewery where twenty tons were used a week, was slashed by 50 per cent. The economy was in crisis.

To deepen the gloom the Mumbles Lifeboat was lost. Five of the eight-man crew lost at sea were members of the Oystermouth Social Club and the board decided to send 25 guineas to the fund opened by the Lord Mayor of Swansea in aid of the dependants. A dance was held at the Langland Bay Hotel in support of the fund.

In April the brewery needed emergency repair work after water tanks over the bottling hall started 'leaking badly' and then a storm damaged the roof. This patch and mend policy cost £1,500 and the finance committee strongly recommended that the company must push ahead with the 'long-term policy' of building a new brewery capable of brewing 2,000 barrels a week. The board agreed and increased the price of beer by £1 a barrel to build up the necessary funds.

In May there was a little cheer. The restrictions on beer gravity were removed. The board resolved to increase the beer's strength 'but so as not to interfere with the present weekly output'. The policy of quantity before quality remained, while brewing materials continued to be scarce. The company could still not accept new accounts. When Tylorstown Workmen's Club informed the firm in July that they had started up again, the board regretted that they could not meet their needs, much to the club's disgust.

The increased gravity meant no extra beer could be supplied for the August bank holiday week, and for six weeks from mid-October the brewery had to cut output by 25 per cent to keep within Government regulations, in order to allow increased supplies for Christmas. Thirsty clubs protested. Drinkers were hit again in the November budget, pushing the price of a barrel of CPA and XXXX up to £13.4s. Another budget increase in April 1948 to £14.8s meant 2d had been added to the price of a pint in six months. At the end of 1947 sugar supplies were reduced by a quarter and further cuts in production were ordered by the Government. The brewery was forced to reduce supplies to clubs by 15 per cent in February. The war might be fading but its grim legacy lived on.

Beer was becoming more expensive and harder to find. Even the workers' allowance was cut in half to two pints a day. It was also apparently becoming worse. Returns were mounting at the brewery, with brewer Lee Marsh blaming the poor state of the casks. He applied for a licence to buy new ones.

Chairman William Morgan assured the annual meeting in December 1947 that the directors were agitating for increased supplies of brewing materials through the Association of Clubs Breweries. A deputation of MPs was presenting their case to the Minister of Food. Financially the year was again very satisfactory with a pre-tax profit of £74,298 and a bonus of £54,600 to clubs. Over £40,000 was carried forward to 1948, and the company started to invest their spare capital, buying £10,000 of transport stocks.

At least a start had been made on the new brewery site behind the old brewhouse when a borehole was sunk during the autumn to find a good water supply. A year later in September 1948 the board was poring over preliminary plans for the new construction. It was slow going. The directors were still not certain that they accepted Mr Culverwell's advice that they needed a completely new brewery. The extensions sub-committee reported in October 1948 that 'the whole matter was dependent on whether the new brewery should be built behind the present structure or built and incorporated in the present building'. This was the building Mr Culverwell had condemned as unsound. The problem was a brand new structure would cost a small fortune. By November the board had recovered from their attack of cold feet and £10,000 was put aside in the accounts for reconstruction 'to meet the anticipated loss when the present brewery buildings were demolished'. Nearly seven acres of extra land was bought at the back of the brewery for £1,000.

The frustration caused by rationing and restrictions led to friction. In May 1948 Ynyshir Workmen's Club accused a clubs brewery driver and his mate of taking a full barrel of beer from the club. The police were called in and the men suspended.

The brewery workers were pressing for an increase in wages to bring them up to the industry rate for South Wales. They also demanded that the cut in their beer allowance be restored. In addition they wanted the two suspended men reinstated or at least paid until the inquiry was completed. In June they went on strike, staying out for three days. A transport firm had to be hired to deliver the beer. Only after an official from the reconciliation board was called in were negotiations opened and the men returned to work. A loan was made by the brewery to the two suspended men through the union, pending the outcome of the police inquiry. The wages were eventually increased – but the cut in the beer allowance remained.

In October 1948 Mr Darbyshire resigned from the troubled post of bottling foreman and L Hambleton was appointed to the hot seat in his place. The beer supply problem was easing, mainly because demand was falling. As some clubs were not taking their full quota – a growing number were complaining about the quality of the beer – this surplus could be distributed to other clubs. Some customers enjoyed a sudden flood of extra ale. Aberavon Workmen's were allowed to increase their weekly order from fourteen to twenty-four barrels.

At the end of the year, in which the company made a reduced trading profit of £56,326, chairman William Morgan blamed the Government for the slide in sales: 'The result of the year's trading has not been quite as good as that of the last few years. This undoubtedly has been due to the falling off in consumption of our products by the increased taxation on beer which was levied by the Chancellor of the Exchequer during the year.

'Plans for the erection of a new brewery are under consideration and as soon as certain matters therewith are settled, steps will be taken to proceed with the scheme. A new bore hole has been sunk and an ample supply of water has been obtained which will meet all our requirements.'

LOYALTY PAYS

By March 1949 water from the new well was being used in the brewery. But with no sign of an actual start on the new building, in April the board reluctantly agreed to rewire the old brewhouse as 'the whole of the installations were generally in a very bad condition'. However, it was decided not to paint the old stone structure.

Meanwhile the attention of the consultant engineer seemed to be diverted elsewhere. The Langland Bay Hotel inevitably intervened. A fire in the garages required Mr Culverwell's expertise and during 1949 he was required to examine such projects as a hut next to the tennis courts and the erection of a kiosk.

The company officials were becoming more sensitive to the morale of the men. In March secretary Trevor Williams reported that 'owing to the disappointment shown by the employees at losing in the *News of the World* darts competition, he had purchased a cup for competition amongst them'. The workers were delighted and asked that a director should make the presentation. J.P. Davies chalked up the honour.

Not all clubs breweries were in as sound a financial state as the South Wales concern and in April the company sent a cheque for £4,000 to the Metropolitan and Home Counties Clubs Brewery in Kent as part of a rescue package organized by the Association of Clubs Breweries.

Meanwhile Pontyclun was being pressed to raise the gravity of its beer. A deputation was received from Abercynon Ex-servicemen's who 'asked that a better beer be supplied'. The three-man team revealed that 'owing to their members' demands they were compelled to get supplies from other breweries although this meant losing their 100 per cent status. They pressed the board to take steps to brew a better beer.' The board decided to take no action, but Abercynon were not alone in their views. The brewery was in danger of developing a reputation for indifferent beer, by concentrating on quantity rather than quality.

By June the Upper Rhondda ward of clubs was asking for the head brewer to attend their next meeting 'to discuss various complaints of delegates regarding the United Clubs beer'. The board refused to send Mr Marsh. Penrhiwceiber British Legion, Ton & Pentre Labour and Brynamman Industrial were also up in arms about the beer without body.

That month William Morgan resigned as chairman owing to ill health and was replaced by the vice-chairman, Mr H.J. Pearce of Clydach Vale. Bertie Rowe of Pontypridd became the new vice-chairman and the board resolved to present Mr Morgan with a gold watch in recognition of his services. The next month another man who was to figure prominently in the brewery's future made his first appearance on the board, when Penri Evans was received as the co-opted member from the South Wales branch of the CIU.

Eventually, the clamour of complaints could be ignored no longer. A meeting was held in October to discuss the quality of the beer. The clubs had established the brewery after the First World War to provide reliable supplies. They did not want to be fobbed off with what some saw as poor beer after the Second World War. However, the board resolved that 'the gravity of the beer could not be increased at the present stage'. Instead deputations of directors were sent out to complaining clubs.

In part, the clubs themselves were to blame. They might want better quality beer, but few were prepared to pay extra for it. The chairman of Caerau Progressive Club had appealed for a stronger beer 'even at the expense of a reduction in the bonus'. But for many clubmen, price was all important.

BUILDING HOPES

The publicans' paper, the *Morning Advertiser*, was full of complaints from licensees in 1949 about how clubs were undercutting pub prices, selling beer at Christmas at as little as 9d a pint when it cost 1s 1d or 1s 2d in a pub. The commercial brewers were certainly unhappy. Colonel J.G. Gaskell, chairman of Hancocks of Cardiff and Swansea, threatened to stop supplying clubs if they undercut the price of beer in his pubs.

The quality of the beer reflected the times. It was a symptom of how little progress had been made in the four years since the end of hostilities. There was peace but little prosperity. Rationing and restrictions still ruled. Club visits to the brewery had not been resumed and the company even had difficulty in finding suitable Christmas gifts. The quality and cost of pipes were not what they used to be.

The new brewery was moving at the same slow pace. The new chairman, Mr Pearce, told the 1949 AGM how the plans were progressing through the bureaucratic maze: 'Preliminary plans have been submitted to the town and country planning authorities, board of trade and local authorities and same have been approved. Plans are now in course of preparation for the approval of the county authorities and the necessary building licence has been applied for.'

The company had made an improved profit of £68,054 over the year. An extra £10,000 was put in the building reconstruction account, and the board made a presentation of 100 guineas each to director Mr J.P. Davies and secretary Trevor Williams who had been with the company since its inception thirty years before. One optimistic flourish for the future had at least been approved in November: 'The secretary submitted a drawing from Mr Culverwell for the erection of the main entrance gates in wrought iron to replace the present wooden sliding gates. Mr Culverwell stated that this gate would be used for the new brewery exit.' The gates were swinging into shape. Now all that remained was to build the brewery.

No one was holding his breath. A year later the project was no further forward. Chairman Mr H.J. Pearce told the 1950 AGM: 'We are still waiting to receive the building licence in order to commence building.' Only the grand plans had been finalized with a conference room sketched in over the board room and directors' dining room.

It had been a disappointing year with beer sales down by 6 per cent and profits falling by almost £10,000. Production was just over 38,000 barrels, averaging 734 a week. This was despite relaxing restrictions on club orders and agreeing to accept new accounts. Only £5,000 was put into the construction fund.

The news from Langland Bay had also been bad. 'Alarming' problems had been found in the bar stocks. Two workers were dismissed, the stocktaker was changed and stricter supervision introduced. The chairman, vice-chairman and secretary had to step in to fix prices. The company tired of playing hoteliers and the board put the property up for sale. No suitable buyers could be found and instead a new manager and manageress, Mr and Mrs Hobbs of the New Inn, Pontypridd, were appointed on the retirement of Mrs Murison.

The one bright spot for drinkers had been the welcome decision to increase the gravity of the beers by three degrees after the Chancellor's budget in April. The grey mist of post-war austerity was beginning to disperse. The brewery even ordered 2,500 new waiter trays.

LOYALTY PAYS

If the company had stalled in 1950, it had the opportunity to move up the gears in 1951. The building licence for stage one of the new brewery – the brewhouse – had at last been received. But instead of leaping into action, the board was reluctant to press ahead. The directors dithered. They wanted 'a reputable firm of consultants' to look at the plans, much to the annoyance of their present consultant engineer, Mr Culverwell. A leading architect, Sir Percy Thomas, was consulted about possible builders.

By early April it looked as if the board had gone back to the drawing board: 'In view of the present costs and difficulty in obtaining materials it was resolved . . . to ascertain from Mr Culverwell whether it would be possible to strengthen the existing brewery and to discuss other schemes.' But after a special meeting on 20 April at which Mr Culverwell argued his case, 'it was resolved to proceed with the erection of the new brewery as outlined by Mr Culverwell for which a licence had been granted'. Only one director, Mr Ball, voted against.

In reality the board had little choice. Even the ministry men, in granting the licence, had said the old building was unsafe. And demand was already pushing the ancient brewhouse to its limits thanks to a competitive pricing policy, as chairman Mr HJ Pearce revealed in the annual report at the end of the year: 'The result of the year's trading has shown a considerable improvement upon that of last year although it is only proper to indicate that the improvement has only shown itself since the directors decided not to increase the price of beer although many other brewers did so. Since May the brewery has been working to capacity.'

The company's decision not to increase prices affected all products, including 'foreign' beers. This resulted in a deputation from the South Wales Bottlers Association visiting Pontyclun to protest about the low price for Guinness. The board stood firm and refused to budge. Supplies of the stout were for the first time this year delivered direct to the brewery. Previously they had been fetched from Cardiff docks.

Tenders were received for the work on the new brewery in June, ranging from £94,000 to £118,000. The board must have gasped again. Their licence was only for expenditure up to £62,400. Only after sending a deputation to the Ministry of Food was the extra cost accepted with the help of lobbying from Mr McEnery, the president of the CIU. Builders John Morgan of Cardiff, who had submitted a tender for £97,655, were then given the contract. The new brewery was urgently needed, as the company was having to curtail supplies to customers. The rule that no new accounts could be opened was again in force, and the secretary was investigating the possibility of obtaining bottled beer elsewhere.

At last, on 15 October 1951, the first turf was cut. The ceremony was performed by secretary Trevor Williams, who was presented with a silver tankard to mark the occasion by the builders John Morgan Ltd. The board felt left out and resolved at the next meeting that a similar tankard should be presented to the chairman, while each director should receive an inscribed cigarette lighter.

The next major hurdle was finance. How was the project to be paid for? Another £5,000 had been placed in the building account in 1951 bringing it up to £30,000 – but this was nowhere near enough. In April 1952 a special board meeting was held to consider increasing the capital of the company. It was decided to issue £50,000 worth of new shares in

BUILDING HOPES

SITE FOR NEW BREWERY

MR. FRANK COLLINS, a director of John Morgan (Builders), Cardiff, Ltd., presents a silver tankard to Mr. T. Williams, secretary of the South Wales and Monmouthshire United Clubs Brewery Company, Ltd., to mark the ceremony performed by Mr. Williams of cutting the first turf on the site of a new brewery at the rear of the present premises at Pontyclun. Mr. H. J. Pearce (chairman of the brewery company) stands at the rear.

THE ceremony of lifting the turf on the site of the new brewery which is to be built at Pontyclun by the South Wales and Monmouthshire United Clubs Brewery Company, Ltd., was performed yesterday by Mr. T. Williams (secretary to the company).

Mr. Williams said the occasion marked another milestone in the history of the clubs' brewery in South Wales. When completed the new brewery would rank as one of the finest in the country.

Silver tankard

On behalf of the builders, John Morgan (Builders) Ltd., Cardiff, Mr. Frank Collins, a director of the firm, presented Mr. Williams with a silver tankard.

Mr. H. J. Pearce (chairman of the directors) presided at the ceremony and at the lunch which followed. He thanked Mr. S. Culverwell, consulting engineer to his company, for his work in connection with the new enterprise.

Mr. Frank Edwards (chairman of the Llantrisant and Llantwit Fardre Rural Council) said the status of clubs had changed beyond all recognition. They were no longer regarded as places where people went solely to drink, but were a part of the educational system.

Among those present were the following directors of the United Clubs' Brewery Company, Messrs. William Morgan, Fred Rossiter, D. G. Ball, A. P. Glanville, Arthur Davies, David Evans, John Brown, E. Ll. Rees, Frederick Adlan and James Douglas.

The firm of John Morgan (Builders, Ltd., was represented by Messrs. J. A. Crone and Frank Collins (directors), Mr. J. D. Gilbert, chief quantity surveyor, Mr. T. Penn, transport manager, Mr. Bryn Williams and Mr. John MacKenzie, site agent. Others present were Major E. Gwyn Davies, M.C. (solicitor to the United Clubs' Company), Mr. Frank Hobbs and Mr. P. B. Clark.

The site of the new brewery is in a field at the back of the present brewery, at Pontyclun, and when completed its capacity will be three times greater than that of the present brewery.

FIRST CUT: Secretary Trevor Williams receives a silver tankard from building director Frank Collins to mark the lifting of the first turf for the new brewery on 15 October 1951. Chairman H.J. Pearce looks on in this cutting from the Western Mail

December; these were fully subscribed by January, with clubs taking the lion's share of over 36,000. This was still far from enough and in February 1953 the company approached, through a deputation to Newcastle, the Northern Clubs Federation Brewery about the possibility of a loan. After 'a long interview' the Federation agreed to loan £90,000 on the security of the deeds of all the company's properties. The Pontyclun company's own bank, the Midland, loaned a further £30,000. The Co-operative Bank had also been approached, but their terms were not acceptable. Yet even with these sizeable chunks of cash, the company was still short of their target. Two other measures were taken.

First the bonus paid to clubs – amounting in 1953 to over £68,000 – was retained on loan. A critical meeting of clubs was held in June to explain the necessity of this action, which was approved by the eighty-eighty delegates present. The relief of the board that this awkward hurdle had been cleared was apparent at the next meeting when director Mr D.W. Evans congratulated those on the platform 'on the admirable way in which the directors' case was presented to the meeting'.

The second measure was to issue a further 60,000 £1 shares in November 1953. However, the clubmen's pockets were becoming empty, and less than three-quarters of the issue was taken up. This 'rather disappointing' result meant the company had to realize their investments in government securities in order to meet the demands of the contractors.

Meanwhile, the clubs could not wait for the new brewery. Demand was rising and as an emergency measure it was decided to install an extra fermenting vessel in the old brewery.

TAKING SHAPE: The new brewery from the air showing the extent of the buildings

This increased total brewing capacity from 900 to 990 barrels a week when it came into operation in September 1952. Supplies from two other clubs breweries were also considered – the Lancashire Clubs Brewery and the Northants & Leicester. Because of all the extra administration, the board agreed in January 1953 to employ Penri Evans, who had formerly represented the CIU on the board, as an assistant to secretary Trevor Williams.

Work on the new brewery was progressing slowly, partly because of delays in obtaining materials, particularly steel. Bureaucracy also ground along at its own pace. The building licence for part two of the scheme was not approved until May 1953. Progress was seriously hindered by the original builders John Morgan withdrawing from the contract early in November 1953; Taylor of Treforest agreed to complete the work on stage one, having won the contract for stage two after John Morgan refused to tender.

There had been friction between the clubs brewery and its original builders over the delays. John Morgan bowed out with the comment in a letter: 'While we cannot agree with your remarks, it is fully appreciated that the congestion on this site is not conducive to speedy working. In the best interests of all parties we are prepared to consider your suggestion that the remainder of the work be handed over to the new contractors, subject of course to our account for the work completed up to date being settled in full with the minimum of delay.' The brewery agreed to pay them off.

The brewery building had by then been completed with the exception of some holes in the walls to allow the boilers and brewing plant to be installed. Essential pipework and

GRAND DESIGN: The gleaming copper and mash tun in the new brewery

ON THE MOVE: Part of the plant like some fermenting vessels had to be moved over from the old brewery

ROLLING INTO ACTION: Washing casks in the new brewery

power was being fitted. It had been hoped to start production at the end of 1953, but now this was put back to 1954.

The clubs brewery was desperate for beer to start flowing from the new plant. Despite using every inch of space and pushing the vessels to the limit, the old brewhouse was barely coping with demand. It was literally creaking at the seams, and tie-bars had to be added to stop the walls collapsing.

Eventually, on 9 March 1954, the first brew was successfully put through the new plant. It had been a long hard road, which turned very rocky at the end with the change of contractors and the need to move vessels from the old brewhouse to the new building. As chairman Mr H.J. Pearce told the 1954 AGM, there had been many problems, 'particularly during the period when brewing ceased in the old brewery and operations commenced in the new'. He added: 'From the subsequent reports received from clubs it is gratifying to learn that the quality and palate of the beer produced from the new plant compared favourably with that which they had long since been accustomed.

'Your directors, justifiably, feel very proud of the accomplishment and the fulfilment of this vast project, and are happy to state that the company are now in a position to supply the complete requirements of our South Wales clubs.'

In the new brewery eight new fermenting vessels had been installed with a capacity of 200 barrels each. This meant that with the eleven vessels transferred from the old brewhouse, the clubs concern could brew 2,600 barrels a week, almost three times the previous capacity. The emphasis suddenly switched from limiting club orders – over Christmas many customers had complained of shortages – to urgently seeking more business. Circulars were sent out inviting extra orders. Fresh accounts were welcome. Hundreds of new barrels were bought. Only days after the new plant had started brewing, the secretary 'had impressed on the board to make every effort to obtain new trade'. It was vital if the company was to pay off the huge loans it had shouldered.

At the end of the year – when the new administrative block had also been completed – the directors were pleased to report record sales of 52,636 barrels, a weekly average of over 1,000 barrels. But trade would have to keep going sharply up if the company was to meet all its heavy financial commitments.

It was make or break time.

Champion Years

1955–1966

The opening of the new brewery was to pave the way for the clubs brewery's finest years – a period of unprecedented expansion. Two key figures were to play a major part in this success. The first was Bertie Rowe of Pontypridd, who became chairman in 1956. The second was Penri Evans, who was appointed secretary the same year and went on to become the company's first managing director in 1966.

Mr Rowe, a chartered accountant, used his professional expertise to keep the company steady during a period of rapid progress. From 1957 to 1967, when he retired as chairman, trade more than doubled. More significantly, profits shot up at a faster rate, trebling in his first seven years from £80,000 in 1956 to nearly £250,000 in 1963. Then the profit figures went through the roof, topping £300,000 in 1964 and £350,000 in 1965.

It was a remarkable achievement, particularly since he had taken office at a time 'when trade was stagnant and competition from private breweries was being intensified,' according to the Golden Jubilee booklet produced by the brewery in 1969. The statement hid the full story. The brewery was not so much in the doldrums as in crisis.

The dust had barely settled on the new brewery and its inevitable teething troubles, when the company was hit by a troubled summer in 1955. When Sydney Lavers officially opened the new plant in a blaze of publicity on 25 June, there was already a growing chorus of complaints from the clubs about the condition of the beer. The board minutes of 20 June 1955 record: 'A letter was read from Ton Pentre Labour Club complaining about the beer supplied over a long period and that members were complaining this week that it was very bad.' It was not an isolated complaint and specialist analysts had already been called in during April and May. Head brewer Lee Marsh was not popular with the board. Even his appointment of a new boilerman was overruled.

By July, the situation had worsened, with one club boycotting the brewery's beer. Director Mr E.L.Rees told the board meeting on 25 July that he had visited Uplands Workmen's Club to investigate. 'He stated that members would not support their previous decision to deal 100 per cent with the company and that the members were drinking flagon beer (beer from two-pint bottles). As the takings had dropped considerably the committee had had to revert to their previous traders as the flagon trade was not economical. The secretary reported that he had since received a letter asking that the empties should be collected and that the club had only ordered Guinness stout.'

Two other directors had visited another club, Marxian Workmen's, to assure the committee that urgent steps were being taken to prevent any recurrence of bad beer. No one was convinced, least of all the brewery directors. During the board meeting they took the unusual step of ruling that for future brewery visits 'a case of bottled beer and a case of Guinness stout be provided . . . but should only be issued in the event of members particularly asking for them'. In other words, when the brewery's draught beer was too poor to drink.

The position was much more than a temporary embarrassment. The then secretary Trevor Williams told the board that the position was 'very serious'. Trade was falling fast. Since the previous meeting he had received fourteen complaints from clubs. He produced another telling set of figures – the amount of beer sent back to the brewery. In the six months from October 1954 to March 1955, the average amount of beer returned to the brewery was under 50 barrels a month. In April the returns had shot up to 99 barrels. In June 135 barrels were sent back. In the first three weeks of July the figure had already reached 104 barrels. The board resolved to hold an emergency meeting with the head brewer on 6 August.

At that meeting 'the secretary read a prepared statement pointing out the serious position in connection with the decrease in trade and also the large quantity of beers returned'. Mr Williams suggested appointing a general manager and an experienced maintenance engineer, but the emergency meeting refused to consider this as 'these items were not on the agenda'.

The head brewer was then called in and the chairman, Mr H.J.Pearce, told him that the board 'were very perturbed' by the situation. Mr Marsh made a number of practical proposals.

EMPTY FEELING: Business slumped in the new brewery after problems with the beer

His prime concern was the effect of the sizzling summer. 'Mr Marsh stated that owing to the hot weather he had experienced considerable difficulty in getting the proper temperature of the water from the cold liquor tanks on the roof and suggested that they be insulated. He further suggested that tarpaulins should be used by all lorries.'

These suggestions were accepted by the board, though later, despite Mr Marsh's pleas, the insulation of the cold liquor tanks was deferred when the estimates were received. He was also concerned about the temperature in the bottle stores and tank room. This was hardly surprising since in July there had been a 'heavy loss' of thirty-seven barrels of beer in the bottling plant (at a time when the brewery bottled little more than 120 barrels a month). In addition, Mr Marsh had contacted the company's malt suppliers, Bairds, about the high moisture content of the malt room, and they had made a number of suggestions including the building of a dividing wall. The board agreed these alterations should be carried out.

These limited measures – but more likely the return of cooler weather – meant the beer improved and the complaints dropped away. The immediate crisis was averted, but some damage was permanent. The secretary of the Uplands Workmen's Club reported in October that 'although he had done his utmost to sell club beer, the members preferred other beers and he regretted his efforts were of no avail'.

This was the struggling concern vice-chairman Bertie Rowe had to lead when Mr Pearce fell ill in May 1956. Only the previous month the chairman and secretary had gone cap in hand to Newcastle to seek financial assistance from the Northern Clubs Federation Brewery in order to provide credit to clubs. These loans were vital in order to hang on to trade.

When Mr Rowe took charge the axe fell rapidly. In June the bottling foreman and the cellar foreman were both dismissed. The sackings were so swift that the board had to appeal to other clubs breweries for the temporary loan of replacements.

The cash crisis was underlined by a decision to ask for a reduction in professional fees 'in view of the company's financial position'. It was also decided to sell the bottling foreman's house in Llantrisant Road. The dominant position of the NCF was illustrated by the fact that the Newcastle brewery had to approve the sale. They agreed only on condition that the proceeds were used to reduce the mortgage account with them.

When NCF's chairman Sydney Lavers came to South Wales that autumn he was treated like visiting royalty, with lavish entertainment. He was much too important to risk upsetting. Mr Lavers helped in other ways. He sent down his own bottling foreman from Newcastle to run the rule over Pontyclun's troubled plant.

The board had long been concerned about their professional salesmen, whom they felt never made enough effort to sell their beer to clubs. Some of the directors believed they could do a better job themselves. When one of the two travellers died in 1955, he was temporarily replaced by a leading clubman. The second was sacked early in 1956, with one of the directors taking over on a trial basis. In September it was decided to make this new approach permanent, with the brewery's trading area split up into six, with each region the responsibility of a leading clubman. Two of the first six part-time appointments – Mr E.L.Rees and Mr E.Morgan – were also directors. They were to be paid £250 a year plus expenses, and were expected to visit all their clubs at least once a month.

TOP MAN: *Sydney Lavers was the godfather of the clubs brewery movement. He resigned as Labour MP for Barnard Castle to become chairman of the Northern Clubs Federation Brewery of Newcastle in 1951*

They might not be professional full-time salesmen, but this friendly old pals act was to prove highly effective in gaining business in the comradely world of clubs – once the system had settled down. In the first month of operation, the finance committee 'viewed with alarm the amount spent by travellers in their visits, and recommended that instructions be drawn up setting forth the amount to be distributed'.

The travellers were expected to entertain club committees. At Christmas gifts of wine and spirits, pocket knives, wallets and clocks were distributed. Stewards were always well looked after, receiving personal payments based on the amount of club beer sold. Gifts from pig-skin purses and casserole dishes to stoles and evening bags were also provided for their wives.

Later all the directors were made responsible for maintaining contact with clubs and gaining new customers in their areas. The brewery's horizons also expanded. Trade was not only sought in South Wales, but also in the Forest of Dean, Bristol, Bath and as far east as Swindon. This expansion put a strain on the ancient fleet of lorries, as a board minute noted: 'The chairman reported that a Ministry of Transport inspector had virtually condemned the Commer lorry which was 20 years old. In view of the increase in trade it was necessary that a new lorry be purchased as soon as possible.'

When Mr Pearce died, aged 69, after seven years in the chair, Bertie Rowe took over permanently, being elected chairman in December 1956. Secretary Trevor Williams, who had been due to retire at the end of the year, was abruptly asked to leave early without a presentation or the extra payments originally planned to mark his twenty years service. Stocktaker Penri Evans took over immediately. Clubs who queried the shock decision were sent solicitor's letters.

This surprise move was linked to an investigation by Bertie Rowe into the running of the Langland Bay Hotel near Swansea. This hotel had long been a drain on the time and energy of board members, who dealt with everything in detail from decoration to the price of meals. It had never been profitable and now there were serious questions over stocktaking. Mr Rowe decided to cut the brewery loose from this dead weight. In January 1957 the hotel was put on the market and by March it had been sold for £42,000 to Evan Evans Bevan of the Vale of Neath Brewery. Half of the proceeds from the sale went towards paying off the mortgage with NCF on the new brewery.

Mr Rowe was determined to tighten up the company's finances. He even suspended club visits to the brewery for the rest of the winter 'in view of the amount of fuel oil burned in heating the rooms'.

Other issues which had dragged on for ages were resolved. The old brewery was still standing by the roadside – and becoming a danger to passers-by. Within eighteen months it had been demolished.

The new brewery was also becoming a problem. In February there were reported to be 'defects appearing in the office block' which were said to be mainly mould and crumbling plaster. For a new building, the whole brewhouse suffered surprisingly from poor ventilation and dampness. An investigation was launched into the building contracts, and after a new architect's inspection detailing £1,698 of repairs, the original consulting engineer, Mr Culverwell of Bristol, was informed that he was held responsible for this amount, which was traded off against the fees owing to him.

By the end of 1957 the brewery was not only back on an even keel, but moving forward, proclaiming record sales and profits. This was to be a familiar feature of the decade ahead. And what was good news for the brewery was good news for the shareholders and the clubs. Each club received a bonus on each barrel of clubs beer which they sold. In 1956 the brewery paid out £50,915. By 1963 this had more than trebled to £180,500, with 100 per cent trading clubs receiving £2 10s a barrel.

This could soon add up to a hefty sum. In 1963 one club celebrated accepting over £6,000, with five others receiving over £3,000. Seventeen clubs enjoyed between £2,000 and £3,000; while forty-two were given £1,000 to £2,000. The brewery motto 'Loyalty Pays' was never more apt. The next year the amount in bonuses for the brewery's 240 club customers leaped to £234,000, which brought the total paid out since the scheme began to over £2 million. In 1966 the bonus was £278,000.

'In the last five years we have given £790,000 back to the clubs,' secretary Penri Evans told the *Western Mail* in November 1964. 'All the clubs have used the money wisely and some of them are a treat to visit.' One such club was the Tonyrefail Non-Political which had received £12,000 in five years, enabling them to build a new extension.

The top club was the Bay View Social in Port Talbot, whose members in 1964 drank their way through 900,000 pints to receive a bonus of £6,684, double their nearest rival. This new club had four bars and nineteen beer engines serving the three club beers. Ten were for CPA, five for SBB and four for 4X. The club celebrated by reducing the price of a pint over Christmas.

The other seven clubs which earned more than £3,000 in bonuses in 1964 were Treorchy Social, Penygraig Labour, Caerau Progressive, Aberaman Ex-Servicemen's, Bedwas Workingmen's, Pentrebach Labour and Taibach Workingmen's. Club members also benefited in other ways. Each year a substantial sum was donated to the Club Union Convalescent Homes.

LOYALTY PAYS: The bonus scheme helped clubs expand their premises

This booming club trade, however, put a new strain on the brewery. More and more clubs wanted to expand or improve their premises beyond the capacity of their bonuses. Other people wished to set up completely new clubs. All of them looked to the brewery for financial

SMART FLEET: The company had not only built a new brewery but also modernized its transport using Thornycroft lorries

support. What started off as requests for a few hundred pounds in the mid-1950s soon swelled into demands for tens of thousands of pounds. And if the clubs brewery would not provide assistance, the clubs could always threaten to look for help from rival breweries.

This put pressure on the Pontyclun board to come up with the cash – without at the same time overstretching their own resources. They came up with two strategies. The first was direct loans of smaller amounts to clubs, with or without interest. In 1957 a bonus investment scheme was set up to try and increase the amounts available. The second was for the brewery to guarantee larger bank loans. In return the brewery expected a substantial part of the club's beer business, with preference given to clubs which agreed to trade 100 per cent with the brewery.

The company also began to provide more than just financial assistance. Design and building work for clubs was undertaken through their own architect. In 1959 a separate company, Furniture and Equipment Supplies (Pontyclun) Ltd, was set up to supply fixtures and fittings. A showroom was established at the brewery. The same year the brewery even began to buy possible sites, with a view to establishing clubs themselves from scratch. The first was the seafront Sandfields site at Aberavon.

As the South Wales branch of the CIU celebrated its fiftieth anniversary in 1959, the movement was booming. In 1960 directors reported that they had attended the opening of eight new clubs. Many rugby clubs began to establish registered social clubs and miners institutes were converted into welfare clubs.

As a chartered accountant, chairman Bertie Rowe was well aware of the dangers posed by the growing burden of club loans. As early as April 1959, he was pointing out that the amount of loans and extended credit exceeded £200,000. He suggested no further applications be considered. The board agreed but soon the need to secure more business meant further loans had to be provided.

In 1961 150,000 £1 preference shares were issued to help finance these loans, increasing the share capital of the company to £300,000. But within a few months, by July 1962, Mr Rowe was warning that the brewery's commitments now totalled £400,000. Again a ban was placed on fresh loans and again this ban was soon breached.

By June 1963 the dangers had considerably escalated. Mr Rowe said that the company was approaching £800,000 in guaranteed bank loans. This would look 'very unfavourable' in the balance sheet. The Midland Bank recommended a limit of £500,000. Again a ban was placed on new applications – and again soon ignored.

By July 1964 the company's guarantee commitments topped a million pounds, with a further £180,000 in direct loans. Again warnings were made and a decision taken not to consider further applications. And again this decision was soon cast aside with £45,000 being agreed for a new 800-member club on the Gurnos estate at Merthyr Tydfil.

Another constant cause for concern was the deteriorating state of the new brewery. The buildings and plant committee reported in March 1959: 'Dampness through the external walls of the refrigerator room is one of the most serious problems at present existing in the brewery. Rain is penetrating through this external wall and due to the fact that there is no damp proof course it is passing through the concrete roof on the fermenting room below.'

Two years later the same committee was adding that: 'A section of the ceiling in the

SITTING PRETTY: The board in 1961 had presided over a major revival. Seated left to right are C.J. Davies, A.P. Glanville, A. Davies, R.G. Leyshon, secretary Penri Evans, chairman Bertie Rowe, D.G. Ball, J. Brown, C.W. Bridges, J. Wellington, G. Stephens and David Lougher

accountant's office had recently collapsed and an area of wall plastering had broken away . . . dampness in the dining room was increasing.'

Drainage was also a problem. Sometimes the issue could be too close to home for comfort, as the head brewer discovered. A minute of May 1958 recorded: 'The secretary drew the attention of the buildings and plant committee to the stench emanating from the sewerage drain meter adjacent to Mr Marsh's house.'

Yet despite these difficulties, business boomed. Chairman Bertie Rowe was able to boast in September 1962: 'Tremendous progress has been made during the past six years. Not only has trade increased by approximately 50 per cent but our prestige as a company in South Wales has grown considerably.' Suitable steps were taken to mark this progress, including a recommendation that 'an enlargement of the directors' group photograph be framed and placed in the dining room'.

During Christmas week 1962 two records were broken – for the highest delivery in a single day and the highest total delivered in a week. The brewery's success was good news for drinkers. The company started to sponsor club sports tournaments. They also took action much closer to club members' pockets. Mr Rowe told the forty-fourth annual meeting of the company, held at the brewery in December 1963: 'During the year most of the other brewery companies found it necessary to increase their prices. Although the products supplied by us are superior to those supplied by other local brewery companies, which means that the costs of materials and duty are higher, we found that there was no justification for an increase in prices. This has been proved by the increase in the net profit (up £45,101).'

The clubs brewery's attitude to pricing was a constant concern for their rivals who were not prepared just to sit back and let Crown go their own way. At the beginning of 1963 the managing director of Rhymney Breweries met Bertie Rowe to talk about beer pricing, which was due to be discussed at the next meeting of the South Wales Brewers Association. This friendly chat seemed to work. At the clubs brewery's board meeting in February, it was resolved to follow the association lead and increase the price of draught beer by the same amount as the other brewers. Then the clubs stepped in. The minutes of the board meeting of March 23, 1963, record: 'The chairman reported that the South Wales Brewers had increased the price of their draught beers. Approaches had been made to the office by clubs asking the directors not to increase our prices. A letter was read from the Ebbw Vale Council of Clubs. Following a discussion it was decided not to increase our prices for the time being.'

The policy of listening to their customers paid off. The next month the chairman reported 'a substantial rise in output for the past two weeks'. Their rivals were not amused. Strong-arm tactics replaced the friendly chats, as the minutes of 22 June record: 'The chairman reported that the managing director of the Rhymney Breweries had once again been in contact with him concerning our reluctance to increase the price of our beers. As a result of this it appeared that it would be possible for the other breweries to put on the market a lower gravity beer at a cheaper price.'

This threat of undercutting the clubs brewery with a weaker beer had no effect. The brewery refused to be intimidated and reaped the reward of extra trade. In fact business became so brisk that the brewery had to extend its stores and loading bays. The work was completed in 1966 at a cost of £70,000.

This incident illustrates the isolation of the clubs brewery in South Wales. It was unique and separate from the rest of the industry. How many other boards of directors 'stood in silence in memory of the miners who had lost their lives' in the Cambrian Colliery disaster of 1965? Large cheques were sent to the relief funds for Cambrian and other tragedies like Six Bells and Aberfan.

Relations with the brewery's rivals could be quite abrasive. In 1966 Crown was so concerned by the methods used by Fernvale and Webbs breweries to poach its customers, that it broke off all trade with them. Fernvale of Pontygwaith and Webbs of Aberbeeg were part of the giant Charrington United Breweries, which had been set up in Britain by Canadian Teddy Taylor to market his Carling Black Label lager. The breakdown in relations meant that Crown switched lagers, dropping Carling in favour of Harp from Guinness – a decision which was to have far-reaching effects later.

The clubs brewery's customers were also its owners, and therefore to be respected. One letter in 1964 from clubs in the Swansea Valley, complaining about clubs beers being sold to a local pub, immediately prompted the brewery to stop supplying this outlet.

In 1962 Mardy Social Club even complained when the brewery supplied the new nearby Mardy Workmen's Hall. 'A lengthy discussion took place and it was eventually decided that having regard to the problems prevailing, that we do not supply the Mardy Hall as long as the present conditions existed,' the board decided.

When the brewery needed help it looked towards its friends, the CIU and the Association of Clubs Breweries. In 1965 Crown presented the chairman of the South Wales branch of the CIU, Mr C.W. Bridges, with a chain of office 'to cement the spirit of co-operation between the branch and the brewery'.

Within the Association of Clubs Breweries, the giant was the Northern Clubs Federation Brewery of Newcastle, who had helped their South Wales cousins finance the new brewery at Pontyclun. One of the brewery's proudest moments came when they were able to repay their loan to NCF earlier than planned. A special dinner was held on 26 April 1963, when the Northern Clubs Federation handed over the deeds of the brewery and a plaque was unveiled recording the official opening eight years before. The brewery's directors and the Newcastle committee were all presented with gold watches.

But within the rest of the Association of Clubs Breweries, business was not booming. In fact some of the other companies were struggling to survive. The Metropolitan and Home Counties Clubs Brewery in Kent was wound up in 1956 and three years later the Lancashire Clubs Brewery went into liquidation. Given this gloomy background, the success in South Wales was all the more startling.

The creamy head to top off the pint of progress came in 1964 when the brewery's premium draught beer SBB won the championship cup for cask beer at the Brewers Exhibition at Olympia in London. This was a major coup since the prestigious championship was only held once every four years and was hungrily competed for by most breweries in Britain. It must also have been a welcome surprise since SBB had only been on the market for six years.

Until the new brewhouse came on stream in 1954, the company had been essentially a two-beer brewery, producing CPA and 4X on draught and their bottled equivalents, Club Special and Brown Bracer. With the extra capacity, head brewer Lee Marsh was told in 1955 to investigate 'the best method to be adopted to put on the market a higher gravity beer'. He was also asked to consider a cheaper bottled beer. The cheaper brew – originally Double Six but soon renamed Amber Ale – appeared in 1956. A year later a premium bottled beer called Triple Crown was introduced, with two dozen bottles distributed as free samples to each trading club. Though expensive, it proved a sufficient success to prompt calls for a draught version.

Provisionally entitled Extra Strong Pale Ale, this proposal was watered down when it was realized that the draught version would have to sell for 1s 8d a pint, at a time when most beer sold over the bar for 1s 3d. But strength was regarded as a vital selling point as long as the price was not too high, as an item in the board minutes of September 1956 illustrates: 'The secretary read the correspondence which had passed between Clydach Vale Workmen's Club and himself regarding the statement made by members of the club that public house beers were stronger than club brewery beers. The secretary was instructed to write that club brewery beers were stronger than the beers mentioned in their letter.'

Eventually, in July 1958, the clubs were asked if they would be interested in a new bitter selling at 1s 4d a pint. Only twenty bothered to reply, with seven saying they did not want a premium draught beer. And out of the thirteen who expressed interest, only eleven placed a firm order – for a total of fourteen and a half barrels.

On such slim hopes was a champion born. The name approved by the board in August 1958 was Strong Bitter Beer, though in later years it was claimed that the SBB initials stood for Special Best Bitter. The new brew sold for £13 14s a barrel in 1959 compared to £11 18s for CPA and 4X. Sales were steady rather than spectacular. The board considered increasing its strength late in 1959, but decided against after the chairman stated that SBB was stronger than Evan Bevan's Bitter while costing 5s a barrel less.

LOYALTY PAYS

UP FOR THE CUP: The prestigious challenge cup won by the brewery's SBB in 1964 (Picture courtesy of Brewing & Distilling International)

Following its championship success in 1964, more effort was put into promoting SBB's award-winning reputation. After offering the 'heartiest congratulations to Mr Marsh and the brewing staff for the wonderful success' the board decided to follow up newspaper adverts announcing the victory with posters and handbills to all clubs, booklet matches and a new design on their dripmats. Steps were even taken to alter the company's notepaper.

These measures may not sound much today, but they were a major innovation for a company which until then had barely bothered to market its beers. And they obviously had some success. SBB went on to account for a third of the brewery's production.

BEST BITTER: A dripmat celebrating the 1964 success

An inscribed tankard marking the success was given to all employees, who also received an extra bonus. Club committees did not miss out, being given extra free beer at Christmas. Everyone had a champion reason to toast the brewery's victory.

FIGHTING THE GIANTS

1967–1976

The championship success at Olympia was a fitting climax to the career of head brewer Lee Marsh. Early in 1967 he retired, being presented with a cheque for £1,000 to mark his forty-three years with the company. His long-time assistant Peter Clark took over.

At the same time chairman Bertie Rowe resigned after thirty years as a director, eleven as chairman. A joint lunch was arranged at the brewery with the South Wales branch of the CIU to honour his successful period in office. Vice-chairman Arthur Davies was unanimously appointed in his place. Secretary Penri Evans was also moving up. He had already taken the title of managing director in 1966.

The cherished cup of 1964 marked the end of an era in another way. It had been won for traditional cask beer still delivered in wooden barrels. Now times were changing. The previous year the clubs brewery had introduced tank beer – a chilled and filtered product delivered by road tankers direct to large cellar tanks in the club cellars. Fully processed and pasteurized keg beer was eventually to follow. These developments in part reflected technological changes in the industry; in part the desire of companies to ensure consistent quality by conditioning the beer at the brewery rather than leaving it in the hands of pub landlords and club stewards. Keg beer also reflected the new bitter battle of the brands at the bar.

In the early 1960s the structure of the brewing industry in Britain had been transformed, with the creation of six powerful giants – Allied Breweries (Ansells, Ind Coope and Tetleys), Bass-Charrington, Courage, Scottish & Newcastle, Watney and Whitbread. These conglomerates rapidly swallowed many local and regional breweries. National companies needed national brands which they could market across the country. Keg beer with its longer shelf-life allowed them to sell the same product from Aberdeen to Aberdare – and so heavily-promoted products like Double Diamond, Whitbread Tankard and Watney's Red Barrel appeared everywhere. Instead of asking for mild or bitter, drinkers influenced by advertising began to demand beers by name like Worthington E and Younger's Tartan.

When the United Clubs Brewery was competing against local Welsh breweries like Rhymney, Evan Evans Bevan, Fernvale, Webbs and Hancock, it could more than hold it own. When the national combines marched into the Welsh valleys and bought up these companies, the clubs brewery was faced with a David and Goliath battle to survive.

In particular, two Goliaths towered over the valleys. Whitbread bought Rhymney

TANKED UP: The clubs brewery quickly embraced tank beer after its introduction in 1963, with a fleet of road tankers to deliver the beer directly by pipe into club cellars

Breweries in 1966 and Evan Evans Bevan of Neath in 1967 to form Whitbread Wales. Bass-Charrington snapped up Hancocks of Cardiff and Swansea in 1968. This new acquisition was merged with Webbs and Fernvale (already owned by Charrington) to form Welsh Brewers.

These giants not only had the brands to force their way on to club bars, they also had seemingly unlimited money with which to buy their way in. The strength of the clubs brewery's motto 'Loyalty Pays' was to be tested to the limit in the years ahead.

When Arthur Davies presented his first report as chairman in December 1967, the new chill winds of stiffer competition were already beginning to blow. He told the 212 delegates attending the forty-eighth AGM held at Aberavon Workingmen's Club: 'This is the first occasion for many years that we are unable to report an increase in trade over the preceding year.' He blamed the fall in sales on the Chancellor's 10 per cent increase in duty which had forced a penny on a pint, and the closure of coal mines which had increased unemployment in the valleys. He also blamed the breathalyser test. But his real concern for the future was contained in a plea lower down his report:

'One cannot help but ask why clubs, particularly those which are members of the South Wales branch (of the CIU), do not trade with the brewery which was formed by them in 1919? Your directors are conscious of the fact that the company is very limited in its capacity to provide loans to clubs, having regard to the apparent limitless sums the other brewery combines are pouring into the clubs movement. We ask all club committees, which are considering loan facilities with the view of extending and modernizing their clubs, seriously to compare the terms of financial accommodation provided by other brewery companies with the extra profit margin of £3 2s 0d per barrel offered by our company.

'Your directors are aware of the dangers that face the trade with the continual mergers and amalgamations that are taking place. It is not inconceivable to imagine in the not too distant future, that your company will be the only independent brewery in South Wales. But whatever the future holds for us it will be the policy of your directors to strive to peg down prices in the brewing industry in this area.'

Arthur Davies, a Mid-Glamorgan county councillor from Tylorstown, was pinning his hopes for the future on the clubs brewery's competitive pricing policy. A barrel of CPA sold for 12s less than comparable rival beers. With the benefits of the bonus scheme, which provided 100 per cent trading clubs with an extra £2 10s a barrel, this made a combined extra profit for loyal clubs of £3 2s. But would this be enough against the financial might and heavily promoted brands of the new gang of brewing giants stalking the land?

The brewery also realized that it must develop its own keg beer brands – or face losing the battle at the bar. But the task proved much harder than anticipated, especially since the company was committed to developing tank beer which required heavy capital investment in the brewery, on the road and in club cellars. When tank beer had been introduced in 1963 – following a pilot scheme in Pontyclun Social Club – it was judged a major success. By early 1965 the company was operating three tanker lorries. By September 1966 it had reached its maximum production (600 barrels a week) with the available equipment. More plant was ordered to provide extra capacity at a cost of over £18,000.

Tanks provided a more convenient and quicker method of handling beer in bulk, reducing the need for stacks of barrels and many staff to manhandle casks on and off dray wagons and in and out of club cellars. The tanker lorries were simply filled at the brewery and then the beer was piped into five-barrel tanks installed in the club cellar. The fact that the beer was also conditioned and filtered at the brewery meant returns dropped considerably. Every effort was made to convert accounts to tank beer, even introducing smaller two and a half barrel (90-gallon) vessels for smaller clubs.

But this new system of processing and delivery did not result in any new brands. It just meant that CPA and later SBB were now available as bright tank beer as well as in traditional cask-conditioned form. Keg was another matter altogether. The mushrooming market demanded strong brands which would appeal to the young. The clubs brewery certainly had a hurdle to clear if they were to produce keg. They did not have a pasteurizer. Keg beer is treated similarly to bottled beer, being heavily carbonated and pasteurized. But at Pontyclun their bottled beer was only filtered – and the bottling equipment was dated.

In February 1965 a board minute casually noted that the bottling plant 'appears to have packed up completely'. Hancocks of Cardiff were asked to bottle for them. In April the bottle washing machine had 'completely broken down'. A beer wholesaler was asked to clean the bottles. The problems did not go away. In April 1966 bottling manager Len Hambleton reported that 'the machinery had been very badly maintained so that losses in bottling were substantial'.

The brewery also had another difficulty. Head brewer Lee Marsh was no fan of pasteurization. The heating process impaired the flavour and character of the beer. He told the board in 1964 that in his opinion 'the only advantage of pasteurization was to extend the shelf-life of a bottle of beer'. Any development of keg beer would have to follow his retirement in February 1967.

As a first step – and to improve quality control – a brewing chemist, Bob Smith from St Helens, was appointed in January 1967, and a laboratory set up at the brewery at a cost of nearly £5,000. This investment was soon to pay off. Checks on beer returned from clubs showed some were weaker than the brew sent out, i.e. the beer was being watered down or otherwise adulterated at the club. Penri Evans believed that 'a successful attack on returns could save the company thousands of pounds' by using the laboratory to check all beer returned and refuse credit where they were not satisfied with the samples. The brewery also decided to start spot checks on club cellars.

New head brewer Peter Clark signalled the start of a switch from wooden to metal casks by ordering thirty metal casks in June 1967. 'This would be the beginning of a run down in wooden casks in view of the development of tank beer,' noted the board minutes. But keg beer demanded a much higher level of investment, as the board minutes of May 1967 record: 'Consideration was given to supplying clubs with keg beer. Mr Clark, the brewer, attended the meeting and pointed out that if the directors wanted to supply a keg beer it would cost a minimum outlay in capital expenditure of £11,000 and if a further chilling plant would be required, the possible overall expenditure would be £22,000. In view of this it was decided not to produce our own keg beer, but that a popular keg beer from another brewery be stocked and supplied to clubs.'

The keg chosen was Watney Mann's Red Barrel, giving a profit of £2 3s 2d a barrel. The board liked it because the equipment would be provided free and would be installed and serviced by Watney Mann's mechanics.

The decision to roll out Red Barrel had two significant effects. Firstly, it delayed the development of the brewery's own keg beer by three years, during which time many rival brands were established. Secondly, it ushered in a period when the clubs brewery took shelter from the storm of stiff competition under the shadow of one of the brewing giants.

Watney Mann had

NEW IDENTITY: As part of its drive to combat the giants the clubs brewery introduced a more striking identity, with the intials UC inside a crown

LOYALTY PAYS

been formed by the amalgamation of two London brewers in 1958. The new company had expanded rapidly, taking over breweries like Wilsons of Manchester, Phipps of Northampton, Bullards of Norwich and Drybrough of Edinburgh. But the nearest the combine came to South Wales was when it bought Usher's Wiltshire Brewery in 1960. Therefore the Red Barrel brewers were happy to develop trade through the clubs brewery in an area where they were poorly represented. In fact, they were prepared to lend a substantial helping hand.

The Pontyclun company was struggling. It was reported in October 1967 that their draught beer business was down by 6.17 per cent. Even more worrying was that the number of clubs trading exclusively with the brewery — their hard core of loyal customers — was down by 8.4 per cent over the year. Desperate measures were required, even to the extent of curtailing club party visits to the brewery. 'They have now served their purpose,' said director R.G. Leyshon.

The staff also suffered, with much overtime eliminated by the managing director in November 'as a result of a drop in trade of approximately 300 barrels a week'. The employees were disturbed at the loss in their pay packets and demanded a wage restructure. A deputation met the board and when they were not satisfied with the outcome, instituted a work to rule just before Christmas led by the more militant draymen. The board said those who worked to rule would lose all bonuses and be given notice. The hard line paid off and the workers trooped back with the board noting 'that there was considerable room for improvement in the discipline and control of the transport department'.

At least the dispute ended one old conflict. 'Following the secretary's report, in which he praised the attitude of Webbs Brewery of Aberbeeg in our labour problems, it was decided that as a reciprocal gesture that we stock Carling's Lager.' This improved relationship was to prove useful. In March Webbs gave the brewery a contract to bottle their beer (some 6,000 barrels a year) which meant that the bottling plant could be used to maximum capacity (instead of two and a half days a week). This extra work helped finance much-needed improvements to the equipment, with a new bottle washer and a pasteurizer ordered in May.

But it was help on a much grander scale that the brewery required if it was to develop new trade. Clubs were asking for huge amounts to improve their premises. In January 1968 Glyncoch Social wanted £100,000 to build an extension; Neath Central Club was seeking £80,000. Both were told that the brewery was 'not in a position to provide assistance for this considerable sum'.

Instead Penri Evans was watching the pennies. In particular he was alarmed at the way clubs were 'gradually extending the time taken to pay their monthly accounts'. Some £23,000 was outstanding in April 1968 beyond the normal credit allowed. The directors agreed to contact guilty clubs and in bad cases to charge interest.

The annual accounts in October showed that the bulk beer trade was down 2,500 barrels over the year. Profits were marginally lower at £322,827 compared to £336,276 the previous year. The position would have been much worse without the economies introduced by Penri Evans. In November the company was considering asking for a bank overdraft of £100,000 – if it could get round Government restrictions on credit. The brewery had already distributed £162,962 in loans during 1968. It was decided no more could be provided for the time being.

NEW LIVERY: The new identity introduced in 1969 to mark the company's fiftieth anniversary even took over the beer tankers

JEWEL IN THE CROWN: Gilfach Goch Social Club, one of the many clubs in the area committed to the Crown Brewery

Then Watney came to the rescue. The London brewers had already offered the clubs brewery some second-hand plant. Now, after discussions in the spring, they agreed in June 1969 to loan £100,000 at 6 per cent interest repayable over five years. The money was to be used to secure more trade through loans. The cordial relationship was sealed by Watney inviting the clubs brewery directors to Ascot in July.

The agreement meant that the United Clubs Brewery could enjoy its fiftieth anniversary that summer with better heart and more confidence in the future. An evening dinner was held on Friday, 11 July, followed by an official function at the brewery on the Saturday at which the chief guest was MP Fred Peart, the Leader of the House of Commons. The company's first secretary, J.W. Kinsman, sent a telegram regretting that doctor's orders prevented him attending. He congratulated the directors on their 'wonderful developments' and concluded by saying that the 'original founders never foresaw such success'.

A souvenir booklet was produced and there were special anniversary wallets for guests. There was even a fiftieth anniversary ashtray. All staff were given an extra week's salary, clubs an extra bonus of 5s a barrel and shareholders an extra dividend of 2½ per cent. The directors received £50 each. Everyone had reason to smile.

It was a time to take stock. The company had a total staff of 135. The brewery was producing 2,400 barrels of beer a week which a fleet of twenty lorries delivered to around 300 clubs in the South Wales industrial belt, from Coleford in the east to Carmarthen in the west, going as far north as Brecon. It sounded a wide trading area, but as Penri Evans

Jewel in the Crown

The United Clubs brewery might have changed its name, but the heart of its business was still in the clubs of the South Wales valleys. The company's sixtieth annual report in 1979 recognized this with a portrait of the clubs in the Gilfach valley, which is worth repeating to gain the full flavour of this special relationship, which was as much about people as beer:

'The Gilfach Goch Social Club was formed on the 7th of April, 1934, with an original membership of sixty. The present membership is approximately 500. During the first week of opening bar takings were £2 4s 3d, a far cry from the present figure, which is in excess of £4,000 per week.

'The club was originally an old library and bakery. Over the years adjoining houses were purchased, and since 1952 three major alterations have resulted in the excellent facilities provided today.

'A successful club depends to a large extent on good management, good membership and good stewardship. The social club is fortunate to have a combination of all three. It has a very experienced committee, with the present chairman and secretary last year receiving the Club & Institute Union gold badge for twenty-five years' service. The committee are supported by a loyal membership and are served by Mr William George Mogg, better known as 'Billy Mogg', who together with his wife have been steward and stewardess at the club for seventeen years. The grateful thanks and good wishes of the company are extended to them all.

'The Crown Brewery is proud not only of the social club, but of the whole Gilfach Valley. Of the five clubs in the area, four deal exclusively with the company.

'Friendly rivalry exists between all the clubs, and the Gilfach Goch Festival Club, founded in 1909 and having dealt with the Crown Brewery since its formation in 1919, proudly insists that 'The Fest is the best'. One of their founder members, Mr Charles Badman, now aged 91, still attends the club and was granted free beer for life some seven years ago.

'The Gilfach Goch Ex-Servicemen's Club was opened in 1925 and consisted of two small rooms known as the 'Moscow Room' and the 'Crackers Room', names which will conjure up pleasant memories for the older club members. The present club was opened by Mr Alan Taylor of HTV in 1964.

'The Gilfach Goch Conservative Club was originally formed as a Constitutional Club in 1903 and moved to their present site in 1924. They have dealt with the Crown Brewery for some twenty years, and have remained a small, friendly club with a welcome for any visitors to the area.

'The clubs in the Gilfach Valley, each of them with their own unique characteristics, epitomize all that is best in the club movement, but they also share a common bond, along with many other clubs in South Wales, in as much as they share a close relationship with the Crown Brewery. The company has enjoyed a long and happy association with them for many years, and we wish them all continued success in the future.'

This was the heart of Crown's trade, but would it continue to be the centre of their business in years to come?

told the *South Wales Echo*, the vast bulk of the business was heavily concentrated in the depressed mining valleys outside the main cities – and becoming more difficult by the day. 'The trade is very tight today and consequently we are running at about three-quarters of full production. Since July 1966 consumption of beer in our workingmen's clubs has gone down almost 10 per cent, and the reason for this is that at that time a man could buy fourteen pints of beer for one guinea but only twelve today. As far as we are concerned this problem will only be overcome by getting new customers. At present we serve about 300 clubs and most of our trade is in the mining valleys of Rhondda, Maesteg, Merthyr, Aberdare and Monmouthshire. It's our intention to expand in Cardiff, Swansea, Newport and Llanelli and, at the appropriate time, we would consider going over the Severn Bridge to the West Country.'

He stressed that the brewery had played 'a significant part in keeping the price of beer down for the average working man'. It was a claim that must have rung a little hollow a few months later when the brewery brought the price of CPA into line with comparable beers by increasing the price per barrel by 12s in October. Six clubs protested, even though the bonus was increased by a similar amount.

Among the companies offering congratulations on the Golden Jubilee in a special advertisement feature in the *Echo* was Tuborg. The Danish brewery had been 'much more helpful' over a plan to bottle other brewery's beers at Pontyclun than their Danish rivals Carlsberg. So the

PRODUCTION LINE: Bottling manager Len Hambleton supervises the production line in 1969. Soon processed beer would also be kegged

CLUBS SPECIAL—An old favourite in a new label—light and clean on the palate, a classic pale, and a best seller.

CLUBS EXTRA—A new extra strong pale ale the product of years of experience in brewing for the discriminating drinker.

CLUBS BROWN—A new full-flavoured brown ale specially blended to suit today's taste.

CLUBS AMBER—A mellow light ale brewed traditionally to give maximum flavour and satisfaction.

four of the best.....

In the beer business, as in so many things, some tastes change. To cater for this we have pleasure in announcing two great new bottle beers: CLUBS BROWN and CLUBS EXTRA. Your old favourites CLUBS SPECIAL and CLUBS AMBER remain unchanged except for their new labels. Try them all when you next have a chance—They're four of the best!

UNITED CLUBS BREWERY

FOUR OF THE BEST: The brewery's bottled beers were revamped and relaunched in 1970 clubs brewery switched brands. Penri Evans had another reason to be grateful to Tuborg. The company had agreed to provide his son Ceri, who had just joined the clubs brewery as a trainee accountant, with a training period at their headquarters in Copenhagen.

The fiftieth anniversary year ended on a high note with the brewery able to announce that well over three million pounds had now been distributed to clubs in bonuses since the scheme began, with more than £1.3 million paid out in the past five years alone. A record figure of £283,272 had been recorded for 1969. But finances were still tight with another clampdown on new club loans. The board supported the South Wales Brewers Association in a further price rise, adding an extra 16s a barrel immediately after Christmas. The clubs were far from happy. The chairman had to address a meeting of Swansea Valley clubs about the rising price of a pint at the beginning of January, while at the end of the month the board refused to receive a delegation representing six clubs led by Gilfach Goch Social.

The special relationship with clubs, so praised during the fiftieth anniversary celebrations, was in danger of breaking down. The clubs felt let down over pricing – and loans. Mid-Rhondda Central was 'very upset' when an application for £10,000 was turned down. In turn the board felt many clubs were taking advantage of the brewery by refusing to pay their bills on time. Penri Evans claimed in January 1970 that the company was losing the use of £276,803 through clubs delaying settling their accounts. This 'had a cramping effect on the expansion of the company', he told the board. He also feared that many clubs were in serious financial difficulties.

At this critical time the board finally decided to take the plunge and brew their own keg beer. The decision was triggered by the increasing number of previously loyal clubs which were taking keg beers from other breweries. Scottish & Newcastle were pushing Tartan hard. The decision to brew keg was a major investment – the cost of the new machinery and kegs alone was £36,638. In addition, in order to promote the new beer, two full-time travellers were appointed during the year.

Crown Keg was launched at the beginning of December 1970 in the same lower price range as Tartan (£7 2s 6d for 11 gallons). Penri Evans said the success 'had exceeded all expectations'. The board were hoping for sales of 100 barrels a week. They topped that. 'Installations had been made in seventy-four clubs and the total number of kegs sold in fifteen days was 1,014,' Penri Evans told the board meeting on 19 December. He believed extra equipment would be needed 'very soon'.

By March 1971 the company was admitting that it would have to enlarge the keg filling plant from its 400-barrels a week capacity 'if trade expanded as quickly as it had in the past three months'. A promotional campaign at twelve tasting sessions, involving 257 clubs, ensured Crown Keg continued to sparkle. The promotion, which resulted in twenty-three new club customers, featured an edited screening of Wales's rugby Triple Crown success that year. In May the company decided to extend the keg plant at a cost of £5,600. An extra 500 kegs were also ordered.

By the summer of 1972 the kegging capacity had been increased to 1,000 barrels a week and the company was also kegging two lagers from other breweries, Harp and Tuborg. A premium keg bitter of their own called Sovereign was launched early in 1973.

The bottled beers were not neglected. The brewery made a point of promoting their newly pasteurized bottled beers in 1970, with Triple Crown renamed Clubs Extra. Brown Bracer had already been renamed Clubs Brown Ale in 1968. In addition, from August 1970 the brewery was bottling other brewers' beers like Mackeson for Whitbread. A special neck-labelling machine had to be bought to bottle Double Diamond.

Meanwhile the untreated beer was sending everyone rushing to the toilets. Head brewer Peter Clark had to admit to the board in March 1971 that 'there appeared to be grounds for the criticism of the purging effect of the beer'. He blamed contamination of the well water and proposed sending out hundreds of samples of treated bottled beer. But the board were reluctant to risk publicity on this issue. 'Following a discussion it was decided that it would not be in the best interests of the company if a large-scale experiment were conducted, and it was therefore decided to curtail the scope of the test.'

The beer problems could not have come at a worse time. The Midlands Clubs Brewery of Leicester had run into financial problems and closed in 1969. The new market Penri Evans had been looking for was open and up for grabs.

In June 1971 clubs in Redditch requested beer from Pontyclun. The board arranged to meet the South West Midlands Clubs Association in September and the same month met ten interested clubs in the East Midlands. The prospects looked promising and the two sales reps were instructed to tour the region looking for business.

By January 1972 Ceri Evans, who had been appointed company secretary in March 1971, was able to tell the board that 'we are now obtaining consistent orders from the Birmingham and Redditch area'. The clubs included Bromsgrove Labour and Greenlands Social in Birmingham which were each taking seven barrels a week. In March he said that the West Midlands trade 'was now prospering' and visited the region the following month, persuading the West Midlands secretary of the CIU, Mr O.E. Cotterell, to become a part-time sales representative for the brewery. Ceri Evans was excited. As the board minutes record, 'the potential trading in this area could be quite substantial'. A 'taste-in' for clubs was held in East Birmingham in May. The following month ten more clubs in Britain's second largest city had opened accounts with Pontyclun. A new accountant was appointed to allow the secretary more time to develop this promising market. Prospects were described as 'extremely good'.

A full-page advert was taken in the July issue of the *Club Journal* announcing that the South Wales clubs brewery now supplied the Midlands. Clubs in Southampton were also hammering on the door, but the brewery turned them down as the problems of distributing the beer in Hampshire were thought to be 'too great'. The advert annoyed the Yorkshire Clubs Brewery of York which was attacking the Midlands market from the North. The two clubs breweries found themselves competing with each other in the Cannock area.

By August some twenty-two clubs in and around Birmingham were buying the beer, with SBB proving most successful. A new Albion Comet lorry was bought 'for sustained motorway driving'. In the autumn of 1972 the Midlands drive moved up a gear. Four hundred club delegates attended two taste-ins in Cannock and Walsall in October and a special sales representative was appointed for the region.

By 1973 the Midlands had seemingly become an established part of the brewery's business, with club parties from Birmingham visiting Pontyclun. Loans were granted to clubs in the region. Balsall Heath Labour received £3,000; Leominster Trades & Social £19,000. A

> ## THE SOUTH WALES AND MONMOUTHSHIRE UNITED CLUBS BREWERY
>
> Are you aware that the South Wales and Monmouthshire United Clubs Brewery is supplying its products to clubs in the BIRMINGHAM and SWINDON areas?
>
> Why doesn't YOUR club share in the Annual Bonus of £300,000 being distributed to trading clubs?
>
> Over £2,772,889 has been distributed in bonuses over the last 11 years.
>
> **TRY OUR SOVEREIGN KEG**
>
> Support the Brewery OWNED and CONTROLLED by CLUBMEN

PUSHING OUTSIDE WALES: *The company tries to attract customers in Birmingham and Swindon with this advert in the* Club Journal *in 1974*

more sophisticated computer, a Burroughs B800, was bought in April to handle the increased number of accounts and the growing product range.

It was a bold move into a huge new market – but it needed considerable capital to sustain and develop. Birmingham was dominated by the giants of the industry, notably Ansells (part of Allied Breweries) and Mitchells & Butlers (Bass). The United Clubs Brewery simply did not have the resources to compete in this league for long.

The brewery's profits in the early seventies were regularly described as 'very satisfactory' – in view of the increased costs. Sales for the last three months of 1971 exceeded £1 million. The company was holding its own, but not generating enough extra revenue to finance a major expansion. In March 1972 a £250,000 overdraft had to be arranged with the Midland Bank. Prices regularly went up in line with other brewers in order to keep profits up. The clubs brewery only kept a smile on its customers' faces by delaying the rise longer than its rivals.

The relationship with Watneys did continue to provide some substantial financial help. In October 1972 the London brewers waived the outstanding interest of £60,000 on their loan, and followed this up in April 1973 by granting an interest-free loan of £250,000 'to fund the development of trade of both companies in clubs in South Wales'.

But this had to be set against the increasing demand for larger and larger loans from clubs. In January 1974 Abercwmboi British Legion was asking for £40,000; Portmead Social Club was looking for £80,000. The true financial position was shown in a minute of the finance

SPORTING CHANCE: *The new keg beers needed heavy promotion if they were to succeed. Rugby sponsorship was used to push Crown Keg in 1975*

committee in October 1974: 'The directors were presented with a report on the cash liquidity of the company for the following twelve months. After a lengthy discussion it was recommended that no loans in excess of £5,000 could be contemplated for the next twelve months. . . . With the escalating cost of building, it is anticipated that it will be impossible for this company to finance modifications to club premises out of the unappropriated annual profits.'

All the brewery could offer was to subsidize the interest if clubs sought loans from their banks. It was against this tight financial background that the Midlands market began to slip away. The crunch came in February 1975 in a letter from the powerful Northern Clubs Federation Brewery of Newcastle who had taken over the Yorkshire Clubs Brewery in 1973, leaving just themselves and the South Wales company as the last two clubs breweries in Britain. Their letter suggested a joint venture to establish a depot in Coventry to supply the Midlands market. It would cost £275,000 and the United Clubs Brewery would be required to pay £125,000. 'It was decided, in view of our liquid cash position, that we could not involve ourselves in the project,' recorded the Pontyclun board minute.

The decision meant the effective end of the Midlands trade. The Northern Clubs

BIG MARKET: *Clubs in the Midlands tended to be larger than those in South Wales. This painting shows Braunston WMC's concert hall*

Federation went on to establish the depot on their own. All the South Wales clubs brewery could do was to advise their Midlands representative in July 1975 that 'unless there was a substantial improvement in the level of sales in the Birmingham area by the end of the year, then this company could not justify a sales rep there'.

Penri Evans now totally ran the company – and increasingly controlled the board. The strength of his position was underlined in May 1974 when he was appointed vice-chairman unopposed on the retirement of C.W. Bridges (who had replaced C.J. Davies). A few months later he reached the very top when he was made chairman of the company in February 1975 on the retirement of Arthur Davies.

Meanwhile another problem was rumbling and grumbling on at the brewery. An iron-ore mine, two miles from the brewhouse, had closed down, causing the well water to become over-contaminated with iron salts. The purging effect was back with a vengeance. The obvious solution was to switch to town water, but Taf Fechen Water Board said in April 1974 that they did not have the local capacity to allow the brewery to use their mains. Head brewer Peter Clark held a meeting with the county analyst in October to discuss 'the purging effect of our beers and the remedial action which could be instituted to eliminate this side effect'. The analyst recommended installing a treatment plant by the well to provide water with a low magnesium content. The board was becoming nervous and urged in November 'that we proceed with this matter without delay'.

There was just one hitch. The company supplying the treatment plant could not install it for at least twelve months. The board were in agony. Drinkers were desperate for relief. So the board agreed to pay two-thirds of the cost of pipework to bring in mains water from further afield. By March 1975 the brewery had switched to town water, though the company was wary about publicizing the change. Only an 'appropriately worded letter' was sent out to club secretaries.

The clubs brewery, however, needed more than a change of water. It needed a change in fortune. Sales were on the slide. In March 1975 the board had a long discussion about the future in light of the 'loss of trade over the past four years'. The previous year the directors had rejected expensive television advertising, saying it was 'not an attractive proposition for a company not selling to the general public'. Now, with Penri Evans as chairman, they changed their mind.

For the first time an advertising agency – Charles Barker, Black and Gross – was appointed. A sampling coach was bought for £5,000 and the number of full-time sales reps was increased from three to five. Sports sponsorship was embraced with the brewery backing the Welsh Mid-District Rugby Union for three years. The company which had hidden behind club bars decided to have a higher profile. Pubs were no longer out of bounds.

The company was becoming more like other brewing firms. In August 1974 it had become a co-opted partner in Harp Lager, the Guinness dominated company, which allowed the clubs brewery a share in the profits. In June 1975 its application to join the South Wales Brewers Association was accepted. The clubs company had come in from the cold. It was no longer so industrially isolated.

There was also a new phrase on drinkers' lips – real ale. Despite the emphasis in recent years on processed tank and keg beers, the clubs brewery was still surprisingly traditional.

Wooden casks were still used for much of their cask beer and the company was one of the few in Britain employing a cooper to keep them in trim.

Crown's traditional beers were highly regarded, if little known outside the clubs of the Welsh valleys. Frank Baillie's influential book, *The Beer Drinker's Companion*, published in 1973, said of CPA and SBB: 'Both are true draught beers in cask with a pronounced hoppy flavour'. When the fledgling Campaign for Real Ale organized a beer festival in Cardiff in 1974, the clubs brewery was invited to supply its draught beers. In 1975 when CAMRA opened one of its first pubs in Britain, The Old Fox in Bristol, handpumped SBB was specially featured on the bar. Indeed, its rarity in a pub was made a major selling point.

The clubs brewery was waking up to a possible new market. When the company sponsored a horse race at Chepstow in June 1975 – the United Clubs Brewery Stakes – entertaining more than 2,000 guests in a giant marquee on the course, the emphasis was suddenly on their neglected real ales. In an advertising feature in the *Glamorgan Gazette*, the company boasted: 'Clubs Pale Ale and Special Best Bitter (which won the Championship Cup at the Brewers Exhibition in 1964) are conventionally brewed beers which are still available in wooden containers, and the company considers that it might be unique in being the only brewery still supplying its customers conventional draught beer in wooden hogsheads (huge 54-gallon casks).

'Conventional draught beer in wooden containers still accounts for two-thirds of the total production of the company who feel that there is every indication that the trend in drinking habits could well revert to a substantial sale of conventional, naturally conditioned cask beer.'

However, not all directors – or the advertising agency – were convinced. They wanted to investigate launching a more heavily promoted and blander keg beer 'having regard to the success achieved of the national keg beers which have no distinct pallet (sic) and in particular are not what can be termed bitter or hoppy beers.' This view won the day.

In September 1975 the brewers were instructed to produce a new keg beer 'having a full pallet, but of a bland acceptable nature, taking all the necessary steps to eliminate the existing tangy, bitter pallet of our existing beers.' Some directors wanted to remove the tangy taste from all the beers, saying it was 'no longer acceptable to the majority of the younger drinkers'.

It was agreed in October that the South Wales and Monmouthshire United Clubs Brewery name was also too much of a mouthful. A new company image was needed. The results of this thinking appeared in 1976. The new bland keg beer Great Western was launched in March at a cost of almost £150,000. Promotion was much heavier than for the previous keg beers, ranging from dripmats, bar cloths and badged glasses to television advertising featuring the steam engine, *King George V*. Much was riding on the new brew. Weekly production was down to 1,174 barrels.

The next month the name Crown Brewery was agreed for the company, though it was not officially adopted until accepted by the AGM at the end of the year. Behind the slicker promotion, however, the old problems remained the same – or were getting worse. Profits had fallen by £100,000 in 1975 and at the end of the year the company had taken out an overdraft of £1 million to keep going. Large loans to clubs were frozen and an increasing number were not paying their bills on time. In September 1976 over half a million pounds was outstanding beyond the thirty-day limit. A growing number of accounts were over ninety days late. That month a meeting was called to discuss 'the liquid cash crisis of the company' which decided to increase the authorized share capital from £300,000 to £500,000.

The partnership with Watneys was fading and the relationship with the Northern Clubs Federation was chilly. The South Wales company had 'incurred the displeasure' of the Newcastle brewery when it attempted to revive sales in the Midlands. The board had to journey north in October to try and mend fences at a meeting at the Airport Hotel in Newcastle. The new Crown rested uneasily in a hostile world.

Uneasy Crown

1977-1988

When the South Wales and Monmouthshire United Clubs Brewery formally adopted its snappier title at an extraordinary meeting of shareholders at Aberavon Workingmen's Club in January 1977, there was only one man wearing the new crown. Chairman Penri Evans assured the Caerau Progressive Club that 'the change of name of the company would not in any way affect the policy of the company in its trading relationship with customer clubs'. The pledge was accepted. His word ruled the company.

But owing to an age limit on directors, Penri Evans had to retire at the end of the year – and was grooming his son to take over his position. No one was allowed to stand in the way. When Penri Evans had moved up to become chairman early in 1975, the board had not immediately filled the vacant managing director's post. Mr Evans senior was not amused. In a lengthy lecture he warned the board that 'a vacuum will be created in the management of the company's affairs' and that 'associated institutes are already concerned over the future management of this company'. He believed some people were conspiring against what he saw as the inevitable succession. 'It is so regrettable that there has developed in recent weeks or months widespread rumours, gossip and personal intrigue, which can do irretrievable harm to the company. Indeed, I venture to say that in my twenty-five years' intimate connection with the brewery, never has so much harm been perpetrated against the image of the company, both externally and internally, than in the past month or two. The sooner this is rectified the better for all concerned.'

The big names were brought up. Director Elfed Davies – the former MP for Rhondda East and now Lord Davies of Penrhys – moved that Ceri Evans be appointed managing director. The motion was carried unanimously.

However, the issue would not go away. Some were questioning the board's right to appoint a director without an election. This had never been a problem for his father. Penri Evans had first been co-opted as a director representing the South Wales CIU in 1949. In December 1975 he was elected a director representing individual shareholders, taking the seat left by the retiring chairman Arthur Davies. Counsel's opinion was sought on the issue. It was favourable – the board had acted correctly in appointing Ceri Evans a director.

Penri Evans must have been disturbed, therefore, when in May 1977 director Colin Hughes informed the board that he had independently sought counsel's opinion which conflicted with this view. Ceri Evans 'questioned the permissibility of the counsel's opinion

CROWNING MOMENT: The clubs brewery's new name and crown logo featured in a showcard early in 1977

unilaterally obtained' and Penri Evans said he was satisfied with the ruling the company had obtained. He moved to have Ceri Evans' appointment confirmed. However, the board decided that a second opinion should be sought 'to ensure that the directors had taken all reasonable steps to clarify the points of law raised'.

At the next meeting in June the board was informed that Mr John Davies QC had ruled that they were acting correctly. However, 'to remove any question of doubt', the directors formally 'appointed Mr Ceri Evans full-time director under Article 90 of the Articles of Association of the company, such appointment to be confirmed by the shareholders at the next following Annual General Meeting'. The decision was to prove a fatal blow to Penri Evans' plans and Ceri Evans' career at the brewery.

To underline the fact that his position was far from set in concrete, vice-chairman Denzil Jones proposed that 'a decision on the appointment of Mr Ceri Evans as managing director be deferred for a period of seven months until such time as the overall management structure of the company is determined.' This must have sounded ominous to Ceri Evans, who had already been appointed to the post at the beginning of 1975. The future depended on the vote at the AGM.

Yet he still seemed to be in the driving seat. In July his salary was increased by £1,800 a year and in August it was agreed to appoint a marketing manager under him. There was deep suspicion about how fair the forthcoming election would be. In October Colin Hughes expressed concern about 'undated proxies' as he feared this 'thwarted the right of the shareholders to change their minds'. He had the notice of the election altered to include a warning about this. Ray Long even asked that the ballot be conducted by the Law Reform Society, but there was no seconder for this suggestion.

In November a cheque of £2,500 was agreed in recognition of Penri Evans' twenty-seven years of service. He was retiring as he had reached the age of seventy – a few weeks too early for Ceri Evans. His father would not be in the chair at the vital AGM in January. Colin Hughes wanted the important position and was narrowly voted into the chair by seven votes to six at the board meeting in December. On his last day in office chairman Penri Evans then overturned the decision, declaring two of the votes invalid as they were from co-opted directors. This controversial ruling ensured that his nomination, Denzil Jones, would chair the AGM. But Ceri Evans would miss his father's skilful handling at the meeting.

It was a stormy affair at Rhydyfelin Labour Club. Hardly had the 275 representatives arrived than Gilbert Bevan, secretary of Tylorstown WMC, asked for the AGM to be adjourned, claiming it was illegal as the number of proxies did not tally. Everyone was on edge about the vote. Denzil Jones ruled that the meeting should continue. After the annual report there were many pointed questions about the level of directors' salaries, expenses and shareholdings. When it came to the confirmation of Ceri Evans as a director, all the voices from the floor seemed to be against him. The minutes recorded: 'Mr McDonald spoke against the confirmation of Mr Ceri Evans, indicating that it was his opinion that no director should be appointed to the board without election. Mr T. Morgan stated that since Mr Evans was only in his early thirties with a lifetime in front of him, he should first prove himself. He urged the shareholders to vote against the confirmation. Mr Ian Button thought there had been enough chit chat and suggested that we get on with the poll.'

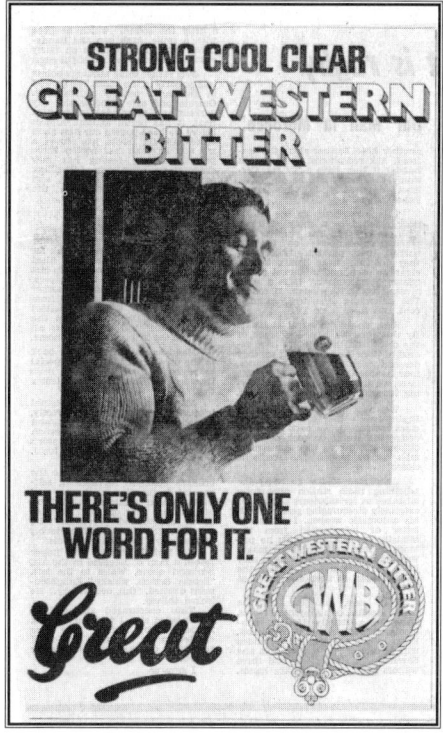

DRIVING FORCE: Crown's new keg bitter Great Western which the brewery hoped would capture new sales

The chairman took this final piece of advice. The vote was almost two to one against Ceri Evans, with 128,388 in favour and 253,807 against. The poll not only lost him his seat on the board, but also his job. He was still company secretary but the new board under the chairmanship of Colin Hughes decided that he would no longer be in overall control of the company, splitting responsibilities equally between him, financial controller Gareth Thomas, who had been appointed as a cost accountant in 1975, and the three brewers. Ceri Evans' contract as managing director, agreed in 1975, was repudiated. He was in an impossible position and left at the end of February, being replaced as company secretary by Gareth Thomas.

At the same time, one new director was attracting favourable publicity. Under the headline 'Ex-bottling boy gets a job on the board', the *Western Mail* reported that Danny Mordecai, who had started work at the brewery as a fourteen-year-old in 1933, had climbed right to the top after forty-four years with the firm. The company's longest-serving employee, he had been a drayman for twenty years and transport manager for eighteen years before being elected a director by 14,000 votes, filling the vacant seat left by Penri Evans. He had always wanted to join the board. 'Now my ambition has been realized, I am absolutely thrilled,' he told the newspaper. It was the first time that a brewery worker had risen to the heights of a seat on the board.

He had become a director at another watershed in the company's history. For the first time in almost three decades, there would not be a member of the Evans family helping run

DANNY MORDECAI: The drayman who became a director pictured, left, with fellow worker Sam Berry while on the lorries

the company. The services of consulting engineer Barri Evans had also been 'dispensed with forthwith'.

The election result also cast a shadow over Penri Evans' twenty-seven years with the brewery. In his final chairman's address he had proudly talked about how the company had gone 'from strength to strength' during this period, turnover increasing from £250,000 in 1950 to £7,200,000. Despite all the problems, compounded by high inflation and increasing bad debts – a massive provision of £198,875 for doubtful trade debts and loans had to be made in the 1977 accounts – the company in his final year had shown welcome recovery.

Turnover was up by more than 20 per cent from £5.9m in 1976 to £7.2m in 1977. Pre-tax profits bounced up from £88,924 in the previous year to £312,546 in 1977. Most welcome of all, the amount of beer brewed at Pontyclun had increased by 13.4 per cent in a static market. This growth was almost entirely due to 'the resounding success of Great

Western Bitter'. Unfortunately, the company's next new product was not to prove such a winner.

The head of steam built up behind Great Western – heavily promoted with special presentation evenings and cash payments to stewards taking the premium keg beer – encouraged the company and its advertising agency to look eagerly at other new products.

The brewery in 1977 did consider brewing its own lager. Crown already offered customers a wide range including Harp and Kronenbourg, Tuborg Pilsner and Gold, and more recently Skol from Allied Breweries. But their main supplier, Harp, poured cold beer on the proposal, saying the volumes were not sufficient to make the venture worthwhile. Instead in November it was decided to renew the co-partnership agreement with Harp as 'it was unlikely that this company would produce a thoroughbred lager during the course of the next three years'. As part of the agreement Crown undertook not to brew a lager in competition with Harp products.

Alternatives such as marketing Federation Brewery's lager under Crown's own name did not materialize, as a reciprocal trading agreement with the distant Newcastle clubs brewery did not get off the ground. A bolder scheme to produce a joint Welsh lager in conjunction with the other independent brewers in South Wales – Brains, Buckleys and Felinfoel – also failed to froth. Advertising agent John Knight suggested Crown brew a 'beer with lager characteristics' – but his main pitch was for another product. This was a low-gravity keg beer to compete with the market leader in South Wales, Allbright from Welsh Brewers. This significant high-volume sector of the Welsh beer business was certainly worth attacking. The beer produced stood up well in blind tastings against the competition. There was just one problem – the name. John Knight convinced the board that the title 'Same Again' had 'substantial potential'. Instead, when launched early in 1978, it flopped. An initial spurt of promotion, including television advertising, saw 255 taps established in 112 clubs, but drinkers saw the name as a short-term gimmick and failed to come back for more. A report described the results as 'disappointing to say the least'.

An attempt to revive the flagging new brand was not helped by a bust-up with the Independent Broadcasting Authority over a television campaign for Same Again. The IBA had cut a saucy advert, featuring a girl on a pool table, to shreds. The company protested about the 'censorship to such an extent' of the commercial, 'particularly in view of the type of commercials at present being shown by other brewery companies'. The IBA curtly replied in September that they had 'absolute authority' to exclude adverts they considered unsuitable, adding: 'It is therefore sheer folly to produce a film without getting pre-production script clearance.' The board's relationship with their advertising agent was never the same again after this and soon ended.

In November the brewery launched Crown Dark Mild into seventy clubs in a bid to win over drinkers in the cities of Cardiff and Swansea where dark beer was still a major seller. But it was the company's original keg beer which took the honours in 1978, when in a *Sunday Mirror* competition to find the best beer in Britain, Crown Keg was voted the best bitter in Wales. To celebrate Crown placed a four-page advertising feature in the *Western Mail* in October which claimed production was 1,700 barrels a week – some 25 million pints a year – with a further 800 barrels a week sold of other breweries' beers and lager. The clubs were still at the heart of the message, with three club visits every week to the brewery where

GOLDEN CROWN: Crown Keg was voted the best bitter in Wales in 1978

75,000 free pints were downed by happy members during the year 'helping to maintain the good relationship between the clubs and the brewery'. The benefits of the bonus system still loomed large. In fact, the amount had just been increased significantly for the first time for many years.

'Because Crown Brewery is a co-operative, drinkers of its ale benefit in two ways. The price of a quality pint is low and perhaps more importantly every barrel earns for the club a substantial bonus – £4.50 for each barrel of CPA and SBB; £3 for Crown Keg, Same Again and Great Western Bitter. For clubs wholly supplied by Crown Brewery, there's an additional £1 per barrel bonus. Clubs can earn anything up to £6–7,000 in bonuses annually. The estimated £300,000 to be paid at the end of 1978 will be passed on to club members as cheaper drinks or improvements to club facilities or premises. Crown Brewery, the brewery run by clubmen for clubmen.'

It was a message that needed to be pressed home. Despite nearly sixty years in business, the clubs brewery and its beers were still surprisingly unknown, even in its own backyard of the mining valleys. In the city pubs it had barely begun to whet the public's appetite. A new advertising agency, Hamill Toms, appointed in November 1978, conducted a number of public product tests of Crown beers against rival brands during 1979. Although three of the five sites were in Crown's heartland at Pontypridd, Abertillery and Blackwood (the other two being Swansea and Newport), there was worrying ignorance about the beers among 450 regular drinkers questioned (a fifth of whom downed more than fifty pints a week).

The samplers' responses when told the name of the Crown beer must have worried the directors. 'What's that?' 'Never heard of it!' 'Whose is it?' were commonly recorded. 'Ignorance of Same Again was probably appreciably higher since a further 7 per cent made other comments about the name,' said the report. 'Only one respondent claimed a Crown product (SBB) was his normal brand, but they did figure more among 'other' beers drunk, the highest being Great Western Bitter mentioned by 5 per cent,' the report added. In contrast 71 per cent of drinkers tested in Abertillery said Allbright from Welsh Brewers was their regular tipple.

Surprisingly, despite many rude remarks about Same Again's name, in a blind tasting it turned out to be the favoured Crown pint – perhaps because it was based on Allbright. There was nothing wrong with the beer brewed by David Cox, who had taken over as head brewer from Peter Clark early in 1979. Its image was another matter.

The research concluded that there was 'considerable variation in the awareness and knowledge of the brewery and its products' and 'confusion between the Club Union and Crown Brewery'. This latter conclusion led the brewery to decide in August 1979 to 'kill lingering United Clubs awareness'. The club connection was seen as a drawback in the minds of the public. Instead the company should develop a new image as 'Welsh, independent and dedicated' with products 'based on tradition'.

As part of this push to build recognition of Crown Brewery – under the slogan 'A Real Taste of Wales' – it was decided to relaunch Same Again with new branding. In September 1980 it reappeared as Brenin Bitter, named after the Welsh for king. But this time there was no television support: 'An original promotional spend of £150,000 on media advertising has been deferrred due to the economic situation in South Wales.' Instead it was promoted by point-of-sale material alone and competitive pricing, with an initial promotional bonus of £5 a barrel.

Besides new beers, the company was looking to expand into a previously neglected area – West Wales. A few years before, overtures had been made to the area's leading beer wholesalers and pub owners, James Williams of Narberth. In 1979 Crown made a greater commitment, establishing their own depot in the town between Carmarthen and Haverfordwest at a cost of £18,500 for the premises alone. A house was even bought for the depot manager. An exhibition was hosted in Tenby in March, a representative appointed for the area and a flurry of small loans agreed for pubs, hotels, guest houses and restaurants.

By May sales were up to sixty barrels a week despite 'still experiencing problems regarding the installation of a telephone at the depot'. A new Burroughs B800 computer was bought at Pontyclun to help handle the growing business, at a cost of £30,000.

The trade might be mainly seasonal and small beer, with many tiny accounts, but the venture was sufficiently successful by October for the board to be contemplating establishing other depots in more distant locations like Reading and Exeter. In 1980 business was so good that the Narberth depot was extended at a cost of £10,000 and an extra drayman employed. In the West of England the small Mendip Brewery near Bristol was used to wholesale their beers.

Early in 1979 the board also decided to buy 'a limited number' of pubs, but progress on this move into unknown trading territory was painfully slow. Crown kept looking at possible sites, then getting cold feet. In 1981 the clubs brewery considered buying a pub company, Honorbrook Inns, but then withdrew interest. The harsh economic conditions did not encourage the board to be bold, with high lending rates, high inflation and massive unemployment. The number of clubs running into financial difficulties was a constant source of concern, with the provision for bad debts having to be regularly increased.

Another nagging worry was the length of time some clubs took to settle their accounts. Chairman Colin Hughes warned the AGM in December 1979, 'Clubs should not regard their own brewery as secondary bankers.' In 1980 extended credit was costing the company over £70,000 and he told the annual meeting that year that 'your directors have therefore adopted a much harder line with those customers who by their actions place an unfair burden on the company'. In 1981 the provision for bad debts was increased by £171,331.

Colin Hughes was pleased that the brewery had managed to tighten its own belt, reducing bank borrowings in 1979 to £145,984 (compared to £449,703 in 1978). Clubs must do the same, though sometimes Crown's tight-fisted policy could squeeze too hard. 'A letter was read from Ferndale Imperial Club regarding assistance in respect of a beer garden at the club,' read a board minute for April 1979. 'It was agreed that this company provide one umbrella.'

The days of extravagant club extensions were certainly over. 'Requests are continually being received for large loans. . . . Too often, however, investigations have shown that many schemes are over-ambitious and that the future earning capacity of the clubs will fall short of their ability to repay the loan,' Colin Hughes told the 1979 AGM.

He stood down as chairman at the beginning of 1981. New chairman Denzil Jones was able to tell the AGM that year that current assets exceeded liabilities for the first time in eleven years. 'When one considers that in 1975 our net current liabilities stood at £1,111,677, the efforts which have been made to improve liquidity and minimize the effects high borrowing requirements have on your company can readily be seen.'

Pre-tax profit had topped £400,000 in 1978, with sales rising by 6.4 per cent the following year. This was at a time of fierce competition when the beer market across Britain was falling by 2.5 per cent. One salesman even reported that 'problems had been experienced with other brewers offering sums of money for our beers not to be installed'.

A key factor in Crown's success was its pricing policy. The clubs still had a strong influence on the board – and they never welcomed the cost of drinking going up. When the board put up prices in May 1979 director Ray Long, representing club shareholders, walked out 'due to his strong views on the decision of the directors regarding the increase in prices'.

Beer prices were rocketing upwards across Britain. In 1981 they rose by a staggering 26.3 per cent in twelve months. After the budget in March, which saw the cost of a barrel leap by as much as £12.50, directors' allowances for goodwill visits to clubs had to be raised to meet 'the increased prices for beer paid by the directors'.

Higher prices inevitably meant lower demand, particularly in an economic depression. Crown was one of the few breweries trying to break this vicious circle, as the price of a pint spiralled out of control. New chairman Denzil Jones made a passionate appeal in his annual address in December 1981: 'It is worth reflecting that if all those clubs in South Wales, who do not trade with us, purchased only one barrel of beer or lager per week from this company, we would be able to alter substantially the pricing structure of beers and lagers sold in South Wales. This would help not only those who drink our commodities, but also consumers of other beers by restricting the ability of the national companies to continually pass on price increases.'

In 1981 the company again increased sales despite a national fall of 5 per cent. This was mainly thanks to their new value-for-money beer, Brenin Bitter, 'which with its competitive price has proved to be extremely popular with the customers'. Pre-tax profits were £346,909.

But Gareth Thomas, who was appointed chief executive in May 1981 and was later elected a director in 1984, was already concerned about the future as the recession bit deeper into the South Wales coalfield. The company was forced to look at ways of reducing operating costs, such as experimenting with two-days-a-week brewing. In 1982 a number of employees were made redundant as sales and profits started to slide downwards. A board meeting in the summer of 1982 reflected the need for 'substantial action' to increase sales. It was close to make or break time as 'the profit projections clearly indicate the problems the company is likely to face given further reductions in volume'.

An examination of outlets where Crown shared the bar with other brands showed the company's beers failed to compete. This was blamed on consumer perception or lack of awareness of the products. Crown needed a flagship beer and it was decided Brenin should lead the charge, backed by television advertising using an 'it's magic' theme and comedian Jimmy Tarbuck. Later, when Tarbuck publicly endorsed Mrs Thatcher's Conservative Party, some shareholders questioned whether the Liverpool comic should still be used by the clubs brewery.

The board also determined to make hefty investments in state-of-the-art technology.

NEW BOTTLE: The Mayor of Taff-Ely opens the new plastishield bottling line with bottling manager Keith Whitehead

More than £90,000 was spent on new bottling equipment to allow the company to sell beer to supermarkets and off-licences in large one-litre plastishield and two-litre PET non-returnable bottles. These revolutionary take-home containers, holding Brenin and Great Western bitters and Harp Lager, went on sale in the spring of 1983. For once Crown was leading the field rather than following on behind. The South Wales brewery claimed to be the first in the UK to package beer in plastishield bottles.

But these investments paled into insignificance compared to the £239,500 spent on a new keg plant in 1983, which was brought into commission in October, doubling the brewery's capacity to keg beer and lager. Derek Dormer, national President of the CIU, came to Pontyclun to officially open the new fully-automatic twin line.

The creamy head on what was a vital year of substantial spending came in April when, at the International Brewers Exhibition in Birmingham, Brenin Bitter won the championship for the best brewery-conditioned beer. The victory was a godsend as it enabled Crown to market its flagship beer under the slogans 'King of the Kegs' and 'UK Champion'.

It also brought a brief smile to head brewer Bob Smith's face. He had only taken over the top job in 1982 after David Cox left for the sun of the Channel Islands to take charge of Randall's Brewery on Guernsey. And with all the promotion behind Crown's keg and bottled

PRESSING AHEAD: CIU national president Jack Dormer officially starts the new kegging plant in 1983, watched by brewery chairman Denzil Jones, right, and David Lougher, centre, president of the CIU in South Wales

beers, he was having problems with their real ales 'because of the extremely low level of traditional draught beer sales'.

By the summer of 1984 he had to advise the board that he was no longer able to produce traditional CPA – once the backbone of the brewery, lovingly nicknamed Rhondda Champagne – because of 'the lack of demand for this particular product'. The sparkle had gone, though a processed version was retained. Crown's dark mild was only saved by linking its production with SBB. Its gravity was increased from 1033 to 1036 and the brew renamed Black Prince. The Brenin boost was sorely needed as trade was still nose-diving. In the same month that Brenin won the cup (in April 1983) sales fell by 15 per cent. Appropriately in June the board decided that the annual gift for stewardesses should be alarm clocks.

Crown's second line of attack, besides investing in new packaging plant for keg and bottled beers, was to move out of the recession-hit valleys of South Wales and head for the bright lights of London where the streets, the directors hoped, were paved with golden pub and club accounts. Opening a depot there had first been considered in 1982. A year later the company was planning to go ahead with the Northern Clubs Federation Brewery of

CROWNING ACHIEVEMENT: Head brewer Bob Smith receives the cup for the best brewery-conditioned beer at Brewex in 1983

Newcastle. But relations were still strained – Federation had asked if it could use the name Crown for its own lager but Pontyclun was not happy about the idea. In the end the joint venture fell through and Crown went ahead on its own early in 1984, opening a depot in Charlton in March. Soon, directly across the road, Crown's Newcastle big brother opened its own base in the capital.

If the South Wales clubs brewery had hoped to break into London's free houses, it was disappointed. The market had moved heavily towards real ales, but Crown could offer only one cask bitter, SBB, and that was virtually unknown outside the Welsh valleys. Even the Campaign for Real Ale's widely travelled research officer, Danny Blyth, had never pressed a pint to his lips. On a visit to Pontyclun in October 1983, reported in CAMRA's newspaper *What's Brewing* under the headline 'Crown tilts towards London', he tasted it for the first time. One drop and he was hooked. 'After a lively session in the Crown Brewery sample room, I was left with a very deep impression and a problem. The impression was of a crew of brewery workers whose faith in the pint in their hands I have not heard matched anywhere. The problem was how to rearrange my own first division of Britain's best beers. This was my first taste of Crown SBB.'

His feature revealed that pasteurized keg beer made up the bulk of the business, with

Brenin the leading brand by far. Filtered tank beer, for a while so popular with clubs, was fast disappearing. Traditional cask beer accounted for a little under 20 per cent of production, while bottling, including the new PET and plastishield containers, formed a significant proportion of the 1,300 barrels brewed a week. Clubs still provided 95 per cent of the trade.

The push by a team of sales reps into London only gained two pub customers in the first six months, and one of these soon fell away, leaving only the Antigallican in Charlton selling SBB. But in the same period over forty club accounts were won, many attracted by the keen cost of the beer and a number secured by small loans like £5,000 to Bromley Common Social Club. A few customers, such as the London Bier Kellar, were more exotic.

There was a third strand to Crown's bid to build business — opening their own houses. The directors had been tentatively knocking on the pub door for years without stepping over the threshold. In 1982 they had agreed to buy a pub in Porth and the same year set up a property company. But nothing materialized. In part this slow progress may have been because some club shareholders did not approve of the brewery buying pubs. It was seen as a denial of the company's origins.

Vice-chairman Ray Long had caused disquiet when he built his own pub near the Royal Mint at Llantrisant. But what really annoyed fellow directors was that the house was financed by Whitbread and exclusively sold Whitbread beer. Some felt this made it impossible for him to continue sitting on the board and he resigned in December 1983.

What eventually pushed Crown into the pub bar in 1984 was Harp's offer of financial help to the tune of £500,000 in establishing a small estate — plus the number of club premises dropping into the brewery's lap as clubs went bust in the deepening recession. One was the Port Talbot Labour Club which Crown converted at a cost of £100,000 into St Oswalds. It opened in December and would have been Crown's first pub except that the month before the clubs brewery had bought the Star Inn at Treoes, near Bridgend.

Closer to home they won a full on-licence for the former Pontyclun Social Club, despite opposition from local licensees. The club, which had gone into liquidation owing the brewery £60,000, was transformed into a showpiece pub for the brewery at a cost of £170,000. Called the Brunel Arms as it was alongside the main railway line, it opened late in 1985. It was followed by The Beethoven in Maesteg a year later, converted from the former Lynvi Valley Social Club. The emphasis in these houses was not only on providing beer but also a wide range of food. 'Your directors feel confident that these new premises will greatly assist in improving consumer perceptions and attitudes towards the company and its products,' chairman Denzil Jones told the 1985 AGM.

But these catering pubs, costing huge sums to refurbish, were never going to provide a short-term answer to Crown's problems, particularly with the miners' strike coming on top of record levels of unemployment. In the immediate future the board had to cut costs again, with more of the 150 staff made redundant.

In June 1984 a list of potential savings was drawn up amounting to £62,000. The biggest single saving was £25,000 by stopping club visits to the brewery. Nothing was sacred. Directors' allowances were reduced by £9,000; annual dinners and stewardesses' gifts were dropped (£6,000 each). Even the staff Christmas bonuses and free turkeys were carved away, though these seasonal goodwill gestures were later restored.

LOYALTY PAYS

Crown's first pub, the Star Inn at Treoes

BEFORE: The Pontyclun Social Club before its transformation into a pub

St Oswalds – converted at a cost of £100,000 from the Port Talbot Labour Club

AFTER: The Brunel Arms at Pontyclun, converted from the Pontyclun Social Club

GROWING LINKS: A party from Crown Brewery visited Harp's Park Royal Brewery in London in April 1981. Soon the links would be closer still

An overdraft facility of £1.5m and a loan of £500,000 was agreed with the bank in December. Denzil Jones in his chairman's address for 1984 admitted that their core business was struggling. 'Our important club trade has continued to feel the pressure of reduced spending power and increasing costs. Certain clubs have faced insolvency, while others have ceased to be the leisure attraction they once were.' A further provision of £254,000 had to be made for bad debts. Though turnover was up from £12.7m to £13.2m, pre-tax profits for the year had slumped from £283,000 to £61,000. And after provision for deferred taxation, the company actually declared a loss for 1984 of £229,000. The dividend had to be paid out of reserves. Crown could not afford too many years like that.

The pressure on many of its club customers led Crown in 1985 to instigate joint research with the CIU and the Northern Clubs Federation Brewery of Newcastle into customers' 'images and perceptions of clubs'. The worry was that workingmen's clubs were seen as old hat and flat cap by the new generation.

One bright spot was that head brewer Bob Smith was able to report in January 1985 that 'cask beer sales were rising and that if the present trend continues it may be necessary to purchase an additional number of casks'. By May his prediction had come true, as the brewery ran out.

The upturn in demand for traditional beer prompted the brewery to widen its range of real ales by experimenting with a stronger cask beer originally based on keg Great Western, with a gravity of 1041. This was sold under a variety of names in the new pubs, like St Oswald's Special in Port Talbot and Star Special at Treoes.

By the end of the year Crown had weathered the immediate storm. In fact it was starting to prosper. Helped by its first full twelve months of trading in London and the first returns from its pubs, turnover had exceeded £15 million, resulting in a pre-tax profit of £206,000. This happier figure had been greatly assisted by 'strenuous efforts' to control costs, limiting the rise in operating expenses during 1985 to 2 per cent.

Feeling that they were standing on slightly firmer ground and could now afford to look ahead, the directors in March 1986 decided to produce a five-year plan, based on the realization that customers' 'traditional loyalties to the company no longer existed to the same extent as previously'. The old slogan 'Loyalty Pays' was almost spent.

In June four main points were agreed. The first two reflected the need to continue to cut costs as demand for Crown's own beers declined. It was decided to cut the staff by a further twenty workers while 'examining critically' all expenditure. The board swiftly grasped the axe and the redundancies came into effect in July. On a more positive note it was agreed to appoint a marketing manager. Of more significance for the future was the fourth point concerning the acquisition and development of pubs 'either by Crown Brewery; by the establishment of a separate company specifically for this purpose; or as a joint venture with another brewer'. The seeds of the forthcoming Crown-Buckley merger had been planted. Crown was increasingly seeing its future growth and prosperity in pubs.

The sharp cost-cutting helped Crown declare an improved pre-tax profit of £261,000 for 1986. Sales, however, were disappointing, as the clubs brewery's traditional market remained depressed, chairman Denzil Jones told the AGM.

'The year under review has seen a continuation of difficult trading conditions. The major part of our business remains in the valley areas of South Wales, which have been badly affected by high levels of unemployment and a slower than anticipated recovery from the aftermath of the miners' strike. As a result overall volumes have inevitably suffered.

'There is no doubt that other leisure activities and changing consumer preferences are raising expectations of the public in respect of higher standards of furnishing, atmosphere, service, food and entertainment. The massive investment by the national brewers in refurbishing their public houses in response to changing consumer demands will inevitably increase competitive pressures on the traditional club.'

At the brewery's annual meeting at the Bayview Social Club in Port Talbot two special resolutions were passed. One reduced the number of directors by five to bring the board by 1991 down to a more manageable size of six from eleven; the second reduced the age limit from seventy to sixty-five so that 'the age profile of your board more accurately reflects the future operating needs of the company'.

Another sign of new times was the presence at the meeting of two shareholders from the Co-operative Club in London 'who were excellent customers of our London depot'. They were asked to stand and were applauded by the delegates.

The old contacts with Watneys still remained – now conducted through their West Country subsidiary, Ushers of Wiltshire, who supplied lagers like Carlsberg to Pontyclun. Crown talked to Ushers about assistance in setting up a pub-owning company called Crown Taverns. Crown was eager to get the pub plan rolling, as projected sales of their own beers for 1988 were down 10 per cent. The company also discussed the proposal with their main lager supplier, Harp.

In April 1987 Crown became triple champions – much to their embarrassment. After the cup triumphs of SBB and Brenin Bitter, another of the brewery's beers won a high honour by lifting a gold medal at the Brewing Industry International awards in Burton-on-Trent. The trouble was that the successful brew was their new pub special beer which did not have a clear brand identity. After a quick head-scratching session, they came up with the name 1041, after the original gravity of the beer, in time for the presentation dinner in June.

But that small embarrassment was nothing compared to the cooling of relations with the CIU. Once so close and cordial – the chairman had thanked them in 1985 for their 'invaluable support' in helping promote the brewery in the London area when the depot had been set up – the two interlinked concerns were now in conflict. Early in 1987 the Club and Institute Union, anxious to improve its standing among clubs and to encourage more to join its ranks, asked the brewery if it would consider all CIU members as a national account with suitable discounts. Crown, having negotiated terms with individual clubs based on loans and levels of trading, was not prepared to accept this.

But the CIU went ahead, proposing deals with Coca Cola and Schweppes which cut across Crown's 100 per cent trading arrangements with some clubs. By the end of the year the brewery was considering legal action. At a special board meeting on 7 December, vice-chairman Colin Hughes, who was also the secretary of the CIU in South Wales, and David Lougher, who was the CIU's co-opted director on the board, were asked to leave the room. The brewery again confirmed that they were not prepared to offer national account terms 'bearing in mind the regional distribution of the company and competitive pressures which would be brought to bear if Crown were the first or only brewer to agree national terms'. After lengthy discussion, it was decided to take no action given the 'limited impact' of the Coca Cola and Schweppes proposals so far; 'the history and relationship Crown Brewery has traditionally had with the South Wales Branch of the CIU' and 'the potential damage any legal action would have on the company's image and negotiations currently taking place with Harp and Ushers'.

However, Colin Hughes and David Lougher were required to give assurances that no information about the company's affairs 'arising out of their knowledge as directors' would be disclosed to the CIU. And the board 'reserved the right to reconsider the position should there be any material change in the Coca Cola and Schweppes arrangements, or any other extension of the CIU national accounts operation into other supplies which might compete with and prove prejudicial to the interests of the shareholders of the company'.

The cosy relationship with the CIU had turned to one of suspicion. The distant relationship with the Northern Clubs Federation Brewery of Newcastle was becoming more highly charged. After agreeing to consider brewing 'own-label' bottled beers for the CIU, the board were alarmed to hear that Federation were going ahead alone, launching a range of CIU branded beers at the forthcoming CIU conference in Blackpool. Even worse, Federation had contacted wholesalers in South Wales and was planning to sell its club beers in Crown's backyard. This move followed Crown's rejection of a reciprocal trading agreement with Federation in 1986.

In April 1988 when the CIU and Federation decided to go ahead with their own-label beers, Crown was told it could develop some brands limited to South Wales or produce beers outside the range offered by the Newcastle brewery. Crown rejected this restrictive sop. Proposed talks on reciprocal trading with Federation were deferred, as it was felt that a 'balanced arrangement' fair to Crown was not on offer. The old trusted relationships were breaking down. Chairman Denzil Jones told the 1987 AGM: 'Since the formation of the company we have been in the forefront of the clubs movement in South Wales. This has been a unique base for us to work from, and this traditional market sector will continue to form the backbone of our business. But markets change, people's drinking habits change, and we have to change with them. Our objective must be to grow our business significantly in profit terms to generate the funds for further re-investment and enable us to provide strong opposition to the major brewers. To achieve that objective we cannot rely on our existing base.'

While he appealed to the local clubs to support their brewery – 'Please consider very carefully the long-term consequences that will arise if you do not have the benefit of a strong clubs brewery in South Wales' – he was already looking elsewhere in an attempt to broaden Crown's business. The London market was by now significant, accounting for 10 per cent of trade after four years. The directors were 'very pleased with the results obtained so far' and hoped this market would continue to develop. But it was the pub market which particularly excited the board – and one troubled estate was up for grabs.

Crown Buckley

1988–1994

While Crown had struggled during the 1980s, another Welsh brewery had staggered from one crisis to another. Buckleys of Llanelli, the oldest brewery in Wales, regularly claimed that it was safe from takeover as it was too far west to interest potential predators. If that was true, the family business's remote security had run out. There were no longer any safe hiding places.

After the retirement of chairman Kemmis Buckley in 1983, a series of speculators took a keen interest in the brewery with its 130 pubs. Finally in 1987 the publicly quoted company fell to a £29 million bid from financiers Peter Clowes and Guy Von Cramer.

But Clowes's financial empire was seriously flawed and under official investigation. After the Securities and Investment Board's liquidation order against his Barlow Clowes gilt management company, he was forced to pull out of the brewery in June 1988, only eight months after taking over. He was charged with perverting the course of justice and bailed for £300,000.

Merchant bankers Singer and Friedlander put Clowes and Cramer's controlling 53 per cent stake in Buckleys up for sale. They held the 8.47 million shares as security for a £7m loan. Many brewing groups were reported in the financial press to be considering making an offer, ranging from Whitbread and the Australian giants Elders (brewers of Foster's lager who had recently taken over Courage in Britain) to ambitious regional companies like Marstons of Burton-upon-Trent and Banks of Wolverhampton. No one mentioned Crown.

But backed by Harp, the Pontyclun company was determined to succeed. In June 1988 the directors agreed 'that our interest be registered with the liquidators for Barlow Clowes'. In July the board was provided with a report outlining 'the potential benefits of acquiring Buckleys'. The directors were already sounding surprisingly confident, discussing the relative merits of brewing in Llanelli or Pontyclun and what corporate structure would be needed.

Meanwhile, the prize target was becoming more tarnished as every day slipped by. Corporate troubleshooters Morgan Grenfell had to be called in to sort out the mess. Buckley's shares were suspended for ten weeks and, after a delay in announcing the company's annual results, it was revealed that a loss of £763,000 had been made for the last nine months of 1987. To add to the embarrassment, it transpired that chairman Sir Alun Talfan Davies, who was also vice-chairman of the Bank of Wales, had been incorrectly appointed. He stood down. Temporary chairman Michael Willcocks admitted that the closure of the old brewery was a distinct possibility.

Like a clandestine military operation, the Harp/Crown attempted takeover was called 'Project Yellow'. In September the bold undertaking was given the vital green light by Harp's parent company, Guinness, the real black knight behind the rescue bid. In October Crown was considering raising more finance 'to enable the highest possible bid price to be submitted'. Offers had to be in by 10 November.

The day before, 9 November, Crown's managing director Gareth Thomas attended a meeting at Guinness headquarters in London, before rushing back for a late-night board meeting at Pontyclun that evening. After hearing a report on the joint venture with Harp, along with projected sales and profits, the directors 'unanimously approved' the revised agreement and confirmed Gareth Thomas's authorization to sign on behalf of the company. The directors were also informed that the Midland Bank had agreed to provide Crown with an overdraft facility of £3.5m. At the last minute, the bid for Buckleys was coming together.

On 11 November the news broke of the surprise winners. Guinness, through its Harp lager subsidiary, had bought the controlling 53 per cent stake in Buckleys for £13.2m, valuing the Llanelli brewery at £25m, some £4m less than Clowes and von Cramer had paid. Under stockmarket rules it was obliged to make an offer for the rest of the shares at the same price, 156p each. The news came as a shock to the industry. Unlike other major brewers, Guinness had never previously controlled regional breweries or large pub estates in Britain. It had built its business by selling its stout to other breweries for sale in their pubs. And it immediately became apparent that the Irish firm was not intending to damage its special standing with other brewing groups by becoming directly involved in the running of Buckleys. Which was where Crown came in. Control of the West Wales brewery's pubs was placed in a new company, Crown Buckley Taverns, 75 per cent owned by Crown and 25 per cent by Harp. Crown also obtained the Llanelli brewery premises, while Crown and Buckley's free trade business was merged.

It seemed as if Guinness had spent heavily – and then handed over its new acquisition to Crown on a beer tray. The 130 pubs were given to Crown on a fifty-year lease, with Crown only having to buy them once they had sufficient funds. The reason for the investment was simple. Guinness wanted to expand its lager sales in South Wales where it was weak. Buckley's pubs had previously sold Heineken from Whitbread, now they would sell Harp, trebling sales in the region. Harp was back as a leading lager in South Wales for the first time since Courage had dropped the brand in the late 1970s in preference to its own German-sounding brew, Hofmeister.

'I hope this will be perceived as a super deal for Wales and for us also,' Harp's managing director Stephen Wingfield Digby told the *Western Mail*. 'We have always seen Wales as a great opportunity for us, if only we could get the distribution right. Now we can.' Crown's managing director Gareth Thomas was equally enthusiastic. 'We are absolutely delighted. This is tremendous news for us, and just as important for South Wales. It has secured brewing in South Wales for the foreseeable future.'

It was an unusual and complex arrangement – but widely applauded. At Crown's AGM in January 1989 the shareholders warmly welcomed the new venture and approved a special resolution increasing the company's share capital from £1.5m to £2m by a huge majority.

But through the misty-eyed optimism, one thing was crystal clear. One of the two

CROWN BUCKLEY: *A new surprise combination*

breweries – at Pontyclun and Llanelli – would have to close. Jobs would also have to go. As chairman Denzil Jones said in his annual report, 'Some difficult decisions will need to be taken as a rationalization of the two operations is inevitable and essential if the full benefits of the venture are to be realized.'

Buckley's town-centre site was the more valuable property, and would have been easier to sell for redevelopment. But the old buildings housed more modern brewing plant. There would also have been a public outcry and loss of goodwill if the town had lost its historic brewery, the oldest in Wales, shortly after takeover.

In the end, perhaps the sudden death of Crown's head brewer Bob Smith in December swung the debate. Pontyclun had lost its champion – though it held on to the greater share of the work. It was decided to move all brewing to Llanelli under Buckley's head brewer Don Jeffrey, with the more labour-intensive bottling and kegging at Pontyclun. Sixty jobs were to go in the west; fifteen in the east. This decision smacked of compromise, and meant that beer had to be constantly trunked fifty miles up and down the M4 between the two sites.

As early as February 1989, the board were warned about 'the complexity of integrating and running the enlarged operation'. There were four companies involved – Buckley, Crown, Crown Buckley Taverns and Harp. A new Crown Buckley name and corporate identity was agreed in April, featuring Buckley's revamped bardic figure, still drinking from a horn but now with long hair flowing over his harp. The symbolism seemed appropriate.

A new finance director, Tim Jones, and a sales director, Chris Oldham from Harp, were appointed. The large free trade sales team included a number of well-known rugby faces like the Llanelli coach Gareth Jenkins and the former Cardiff coach and scrum-half Gary Samuel. So it was apt that when the time came to kick the venture into life, it was launched at Cardiff Arms Park in July. Managing director Gareth Thomas used the grand occasion to present the new combine as the perfect marriage:

'Some twelve months ago I had a vision of creating a powerful new brewing force in South Wales, able to compete effectively with the national companies, whilst dedicated to the needs of local customers and consumers. The Harp Lager Company, with whom we have had a close trading relationship for many years, also shared that vision, and I am delighted that with their assistance and their confidence in the future of the brewing industry in South Wales, we are today able to witness the first stage of turning that vision into reality.

'Crown and Buckley complement each other perfectly. One strong in east Wales, the other strong in the west. One with a strong tied estate, the other strong in the free trade.

TAKING OVER: *After the merger all production was transferred to Llanelli under Buckley's head brewer Don Jeffrey*

We believe this bringing together of both companies, with a long and historic past, represents a new beginning and that jointly our future has never been more exciting.'

He presented Crown Buckley's new range of beers spearheaded by Buckley's Best Bitter which was promoted on posters, radio and television under the slogan 'Good taste will stand the test of time,' emphasizing Buckley's 220 years of history. 'We intend to make Buckley's Best Bitter the most sought-after beer brand in South Wales,' he proclaimed. The massive £500,000 advertising campaign was one of the largest ever mounted in the Principality in a bid to push the west Wales beer into south-east Wales.

That month production of Crown's beers had been transferred to Llanelli after a series of trial brews, and inevitably there were some casualties as the two ranges were rationalized. Crown's Black Prince dark mild was dropped in favour of Buckley's Mild. Brenin Bitter ruled the low-gravity keg market with Buckley's JB and Celtic Bright disappearing. Crown Keg also vanished. More surprisingly, Crown 1041, the clubs brewery's premium real ale, which had won a gold medal in 1987, failed to survive the switch. The Llanelli brewery found it could not reproduce its distinctive taste. Samples sent for analysis to Guinness revealed a yeast infection and eventually the full-flavoured beer was quietly discontinued despite being on the company's original price list.

NEW PINT TO PONDER: Gareth Thomas found himself holding up Buckley's Best Bitter

The launch at the hallowed home of Welsh rugby was heralded as just the start of a five-year expansion plan, with talk of selling not just across South Wales but also along the M4 in southern England, all the way to Crown's London depot. 'During the next five years the company is set to grow. We have set ourselves ambitious goals. We are also looking at every opportunity to increase our tied estate,' said Gareth Thomas in his upbeat message to the press and public. The new company was presented as 'the strongest independent brewery in South Wales' with the aim of 'positioning the brewery among the top regional brewers in the UK'. Such high hopes were quickly dashed.

Hardly had these words been uttered, than the company was experiencing a remorseless slide in sales from London to Llanelli. Trade was not helped by problems in kegging Buckley's Best Bitter at Pontyclun. There was much 'adverse comment' about the condition of the beer. Finance director Tim Jones told the board in November that 'the last quarter of the year [July to September] had been particularly disappointing with volume down against budget and advertising spend well over budget.'

The directors began to talk about the need to concentrate brewing and packaging on one site, and seriously considered brewing again at Pontyclun where the equipment was still intact. But eventually it was agreed that 'brewing must stay in Llanelli for the medium-term future'. The closure of Crown's Narberth depot after the acquisition of Buckley's brewery was seen to have been a mistake. 'The loss of Narberth had cost us business and the re-opening of that would bring in extra volume.'

Crown Buckley was not just struggling but in crisis. Chairman Denzil Jones revealed in his annual report for 1989 that the company had lost a staggering £1,388,000 before taxation, compared to a profit of £315,000 the year before. 'The process of integrating Buckley's brewery and the major reshaping of the group has taken longer and proved substantially more costly than originally anticipated,' said the directors. 'These factors allied to the additional costs of our marketing programme and the substantial increase in interest rates have been the major contributory factors,' added Denzil Jones.

GOLD RUSH: Out to make Buckley's Best Bitter the top brand in Wales

And the position was getting worse. Crown Buckley was accelerating downhill. In the merry month of December sales fell by 13.6 per cent, compared to 5.7 per cent down for the year. Gareth Thomas asked the directors if they wished to reconsider their decision to pay a dividend in view of these figures. The board still decided to go ahead. But prices were put up by £7.50 a barrel (compared to £6 by their competitors) with £9 for premium bitters.

The position could have been even worse. On 3 January 1990 the board was told that the bank was threatening to pull the plug. The Midland had not approved the company's new overdraft requests and the existing financial facility would only continue 'subject to a review by an independent firm of investigating accountants.'

The Midland said the reason for their refusal of financial help, apart from the lateness of the application, was the company's poor results and doubts about Crown Buckley's ability to turn the situation around, plus the high level of debt the company had taken on as a result of the joint venture agreement. The company faced immediate bankruptcy, being unable to meet its commitments to the bank and to its creditors. Once again Guinness had to ride to the rescue, guaranteeing the company's financial commitments in a letter of support on 4 January. Only then did the bank agree an overdraft facility of £4.3m, subject to strict conditions.

But the worldly-wise Dublin giant was giving nothing away. Guinness's detailed offer of support — parts of which the Pontyclun firm was told it must accept without alteration or the offer was off — contained clauses allowing control of the company to pass to the stout supporters if Crown Buckley was in future not able to meet its commitments. This included the scheduled repayment of £800,000 by December 1990 to complete the acquisition of the Llanelli brewery. Squeezed into a tight corner, Crown Buckley haggled over a few details but had no option but to accept. The clubs brewery's independence was almost at an end.

NEW KING: A fresh look for Brenin Bitter

The company was still crippled by late-paying customers. 'A detailed review of those who continually take excess credit is now being undertaken to reduce the unfair burden,' Denzil Jones said in his annual address. Debt collection targets were set and 'these are to be the major priority of the company over the coming months,' the board decided. Loan requests were deferred.

Costs had to be cut again. It was decided to close the London depot, once the jewel in the Crown, at the end of March 1990, as it was no longer felt to be viable owing to an increase in rates and rent and a decrease in trade. At its peak it had sold 18,000 barrels a year, but little of this was Crown's own products. East Anglian brewers Greene King, the junior partners in the Harp Lager consortium, looked over the customer list. At the same time it was decided to reopen the Narberth depot.

The future of the Llanelli brewery hung in the wind. An offer for the site came in from DIY chain B&Q. The brewery workforce was drained to the bottom of the barrel, with warehousing, distribution and office administration all concentrated at Pontyclun by mid-February. Only essential brewing remained. Union leaders claimed that the large Llanelli site was being reduced to an operation 'bordering on a local shop'. Crown Buckley said a further thirteen jobs were to go, but the unions feared thirty-three would eventually be axed, as jobs were transferred to Pontyclun. The smoke of strike action was in the air. TGWU officer Brian Johnson said morale among the workers had 'plummeted to the depths'. He protested: 'Our disappointment is that less than a year ago the company was talking about restructuring and expansion. We were looking for better things and now we get this kick in the teeth.' Llanelli MP Denzil Davies condemned the cutbacks as 'another bad blow' for his constituency. He demanded a meeting with the board. Under fire, managing director Gareth Thomas was forced to give a pledge: 'Our commitment to brewing at Llanelli is unshakeable,' he told the *Western Mail* on 31 January. He repeated the pledge to Denzil Davies a few days later: 'We are absolutely guaranteeing the continuity of brewing at Llanelli.'

The delayed AGM was not finally held until 10 February at Thomastown Social Club. The 374 delegates were in no mood to be fobbed off with assurances. One shareholder, Jim Rees, criticized the brewery's planning. 'You could not have been very far-sighted if after one year you find it necessary to close your London depot. This is a fiasco.' The directors comforted themselves with the belief that after a year of major upheaval and near disaster, things could only get better. They were wrong.

At the end of February the directors were told that 'employee morale was at an all-time low and that both the management and the board were being criticized for continually changing operational methods'. They were felt to be fumbling as the business burnt. The company had already exceeded its overdraft facility and in March sales were 21.6 per cent below budget, despite a large 'Golden Oldie' promotion for Buckley's Best Bitter. Crown Buckley was spiralling downwards, seemingly out of control, and the hard ground of reality was rushing up to meet it. A crash seemed inevitable. There was only one avenue of escape.

On 21 March Malcolm Hall of Guinness attended the board meeting and 'advised the directors of the worsening trading performance, and in particular that Harp and Guinness were not prepared to provide unlimited or indefinite financing'. Harp was aggrieved that the lager royalties were half the level originally projected due to the sales decline. A meeting was to be held with the company's bankers in May and 'it was felt that given the deteriorating financial position and without major initiatives which would enable the company to improve its financial position, the Midland Bank facilities may be withdrawn'.

Mr Hall suggested that the best way forward was for Guinness to convert the debt owed to it into a majority shareholding. This would restore customer confidence in the company and reduce its huge debt burden, while providing time 'to implement the necessary financial and operational restructuring'. It would also mean Guinness would take control. Crown Buckley's directors were reluctant to give away their powers, and desperately sought another solution. Vice-chairman Colin Hughes said that 'the equity for debt swap would do little to improve the company's profitability,' while another director, Roger Hughes, suggested that 'the dual site operation had been a significant factor in reducing the company's profitability'.

A special board meeting was held on 3 April to consider all the options. Before the meeting Roger Hughes underlined the crisis in a letter 'concerning the position of the company and directors in respect of Section 214 of the Insolvency Act, 1986'. In light of February's accounts and projected sales levels for the rest of the year, the company might already be trading illegally.

Though he had given a pledge to continue brewing at Llanelli only two months before, managing director Gareth Thomas now believed that if the company decided it must move to a one-site operation, then Buckley's brewery would have to be abandoned. 'Pontyclun appeared to offer the best option given the high free trade volumes in the eastern region, the overall site flexibility and the potential one-off development opportunity at Llanelli,' he said. Finance director Tim Jones supported this, saying 'substantial savings' could be made by moving to one site, with the larger savings made by moving to Pontyclun. However, the board agreed that continuing to brew at Llanelli while sharing a depot in the east with another company 'appeared to be an ideal solution'.

The candidates for this 'ideal solution' were Ansells (part of Allied Breweries) who had a depot near Newport, and Scottish & Newcastle Breweries who had a depot in Caerphilly. By the next board meeting on 25 April, Gareth Thomas had held talks with both about a possible joint venture – which held out hopes of avoiding complete domination by Guinness. The stout brewers, however, were in no mood to wait long.

Roger Hughes said that 'Guinness's primary intention was to protect the investment they had made in Buckleys and Crown Brewery, and ensure they would receive an adequate return on those investments'. Stephen Wingfield Digby, Harp's director on the board, made no attempt to deny this. He 'confirmed this to be the case' and informed the directors that 'the support facilities from Guinness indicated in the letter of 4 January 1990 would continue in place until September 1990'. After that, if the board had not come up with a solution to put the company on an even keel, Guinness would step in and take control. The Dublin company insisted that an extraordinary meeting of shareholders be arranged to approve this expected takeover, despite negotiations going on with other brewers. Crown Buckley was living on borrowed time.

The board was far from happy and Gareth Thomas was instructed to write to Brian Baldock, managing director of Guinness Brewing Worldwide, 'to express their concern over the apparent confusion over the EGM and the firm view that both customers' and shareholders' confidence could be severely damaged by precipitating action, the consequences of which had not been carefully and fully considered'.

In response, Guinness agreed to delay the EGM while negotiations with other brewers were taking place, provided 'the legal framework for the debt for equity conversion was put in place'. This gave the company a small breathing space in which to consider three options – a one-site operation; a joint venture with another brewery; withdrawing from brewing altogether. Most hopes were pinned on a joint venture agreement with Ansells, and meetings were held at frequent intervals throughout the summer.

Positive action was desperately needed. When Tim Jones in May presented the accounts for March 'the results were very disappointing, with a loss before tax for the brewery of £184,000 against a budgeted profit of £23,000'. This was due to a further drop in sales. 'It was noted that another month of similar results to March would put extreme pressure on the covenants made to the bank.' Tim Jones added that the company 'had continued to stay within its cash targets, but this continued to be due to extended credit received from the Harp Lager Company'.

At the beginning of June Peter Lipscomb, the managing director of Guinness in Britain, came to Pontyclun to meet the board. He spelled out that 30 September 1990 was the final deadline. To extend it would be foolish as the Crown Buckley ship was drifting on to the rocks. 'Guinness is conscious of the fact that the company may be heading towards trading insolvently, and that if Guinness supported the company in such a situation they themselves could be as personally liable as any director.' Guinness believed that Crown Buckley was not trading insolvently while joint venture negotiations were going on – but these negotiations could not continue indefinitely. And if the talks broke down there needed to be a fall-back position. This meant Guinness taking control through converting debt into shares, involving up to 75 per cent of the company.

He gave various assurances of the position if this happened. Board meetings would continue to be held in Wales; the minority shareholders could appoint two directors and nominate a non-executive chairman; there could be a club shareholders' committee. But there was no doubt about who would be in charge. 'The minority shareholders could not have a blocking veto.'

However, he said Guinness would welcome a joint venture with Ansells as 'by far the best option for both parties' since it provided 'the possibility of future growth'. Though he pointed out that 'the major loss to Crown would be one of total management. The day to day administration would be in the hands of Ansells.'

He ruled out other options. He felt Crown Buckley could no longer stand alone, as he did not believe the company could gain the backing of a bank. Liquidation was not a sensible solution 'in any circumstances', while the sale of the company would present problems to Guinness.

Despite Guinness's backing for the possible joint venture with Ansells, the Crown Buckley board was not pleased with the limited time allowed to get this operation off the ground. Guinness was pushing the Welsh directors too far and too fast for their liking. Gareth Thomas summarized their position: 'The board were disappointed that after less than two years of a twenty-year agreement, and primarily due to difficulties which were not envisaged by either party at the time the agreement was drawn up, the actions and timescale proposed seemed to be giving all the benefits to Guinness.' The directors particularly objected to the 30 September deadline and the valuation of the shares.

With the timebomb ticking away, there was no time for leisurely meetings. Within a week Peter Lipscomb was back in Pontyclun on 14 June to hear that Crown Buckley had met Ansells that morning. Gareth Thomas stated that it had been 'a good meeting with a very positive response from Ansells'. Stephen Wingfield Digby confirmed that Ansells 'had been very enthusiastic about the joint venture and saw it as a definite way forward for Ansells in South Wales'.

In view of this positive response, Crown Buckley wanted to delay calling the EGM. The directors were worried about 'the effect on confidence in the company of a proposal to hand control to a third party [Guinness], particularly if, as is now the case, an alternative strategy remains a real possibility'. Guinness, however, were unmoved.

Peter Lipscomb said there was 'a real urgency' to get the fall-back position set up. Then Guinness would feel more relaxed. They had made a substantial investment which was now at risk. The Dublin firm was also not prepared to move on the 30 September deadline. Its support would run out on that date. A swift solution was vital to maintain good customer relations and staff morale.

On the twenty-year partnership which was now coming to a sudden end, Peter Lipscomb said that 'there must be some ground rules and one has to be that the partner is profitable. Guinness could not be there for twenty years with an open cheque book.'

The two sides disagreed wildly on Crown Buckley's future prospects. Gareth Thomas stated that projections for the next year indicated a net profit of £500,000 'so that the risk was already somewhat diminished'. Guinness was not prepared to swallow this optimistic outlook. Their forecasts for 1990/1991 showed 'continuing losses'.

However, Guinness was prepared to move on one point. While still seeing a joint venture with Ansells as the best option, the Dublin brewers also now believed that a 'controlled sale under the right terms would be preferable' to their debt/equity proposal.

The brewing giant denied that it just wanted to seize control. A Guinness takeover was 'a last resort before receivership because of the potential loss of customers'. Peter Lipscomb added that 'if Guinness had wanted to acquire the company on the cheap, it could have done so last January. This was not its intention.' He hoped that 'the high level of support given showed Guinness's good intent'. In view of the limited time left, it was agreed that 'discreet soundings' should be put out to test the market.

Further meetings were held with Ansells' parent company, Allied Breweries, and it seemed as if the desired option of a joint venture with another brewery was going to take off, even though Allied 'were likely to want to put as little money up front as possible'. Then in July these high hopes were dashed. Ansells rejected the scheme.

The deflated 19 July board meeting was told that Ansells had not approved the joint venture because of doubts over the projected cost savings, doubts over the suitability of the Pontyclun site, the complicated nature of the deal and Ansells' 'wish to follow up the organic growth they had themselves achieved over the last year in South Wales'.

This left only one option since no one had shown serious interest in buying the company, apart from tentative discussions with Scottish & Newcastle Breweries. It was agreed that the debt for equity arrangement should now go ahead 'as soon as possible', with notice of the EGM sent out by the end of the month. Peter Lipscomb warned that 'the Midland Bank may now withdraw the Crown facility on hearing of the failure of the joint venture proposals', but he pledged that Guinness would continue to support the company until 30 September.

The Crown Buckley directors were still unhappy with Guinness's valuation of the shares at par, and at a further meeting in London Guinness raised the amount by 50 per cent to £1 50. In light of this, the board felt the offer was 'the best that could be achieved in the circumstances'. Crown Buckley agreed to recommend to shareholders an offer from Harp to convert £3,213,000 of debt owed to it into 2,142,000 new shares making up 75 per cent of the enlarged share capital, effectively giving control of the company to Guinness. The EGM was called for 8 September at the Rhondda Sports Centre, Ystrad Rhondda.

As a reward for all his hard work, managing director Gareth Thomas was given a new three-year contract. This was to safeguard his immediate position since Guinness was already moving in its own men. Philip Moore was seconded from Guinness as acting commercial director, with Mike Salter, a former finance director of Bass Wales, brought in as acting executive officer.

Vice-chairman Colin Hughes advised the board that he was not able to continue as a director as his employers, the Club and Institute Union, felt that it was no longer proper for one of its executives to serve on the new board or even on the new advisory committee. The long link with the CIU was weakened.

Chairman Denzil Jones opened the EGM by telling the 310 delegates present: 'Let me make it absolutely clear that neither your board nor the board of Harp ever intended or wished that the proposals being voted on today should ever have become necessary. All of you, however, are aware how difficult trading circumstances and the economy generally has proved to be over the last two years. Many other brewing companies, particularly the regional brewers, are themselves facing difficult decisions as to their future directions.' He cited the case of the largest regional brewery, Greenall Whitley of Warrington, which only that week had announced its decision to cease brewing. 'In our case we have been even more badly affected due to the unique nature of your company's business which is made up of approximately 80 per cent free trade.' This battlefield had become 'increasingly intense' as the major brewers fought to offset the effects of new monopolies rulings which stripped them of many of their tied houses.

'On top of this we have like many other companies been badly hit by the substantial rise in interest rates, which has meant the effective financing costs of acquiring Buckleys increased by some 36 per cent.' High interest charges also strained their ability to provide vital loans to clubs to secure business.

'Most significantly of all, we have suffered a sharp decline in anticipated sales. First by a decline in 1989 in the South Wales clubs market of approximately 11 per cent. And secondly by a substantially lower than anticipated incremental volume from the acquisition of Buckleys.

'The combination of all these factors has therefore placed the company in serious financial difficulties by being unable to support the original financing proposition and current debt burden.'

Denzil Jones said Crown Buckley could no longer stand alone and therefore the board were proposing that Harp, by converting debt into shares, be given a controlling 75 per cent interest in the company. Harp would have three directors on the new board. The minority club shareholders would have the right to appoint six people to an advisory committee. Two of these would become directors of the company and one of the two would be the non-executive chairman.

Peter Lipscomb, managing director of Guinness in Britain and chairman of Harp Lager, appealed for support and introduced the new directors – Harp's managing director Stephen Wingfield Digby, commercial director Phil Crenigan and Mike Salter who would become the new managing director of Crown Buckley. He welcomed the proposed appointment of Gareth Thomas as chairman.

The top table drew breath as Denzil Jones invited questions. Jim Rees of Glyncoch Social Club described the meeting as 'the biggest event in Crown's history'. He pointed out that the directors were responsible for the losses and commented on recent court cases involving leading Guinness directors and another takeover. He was sharply told to confine his remarks to Crown Buckley.

But most other shareholders accepted that there was no alternative to the plan put before them and welcomed Guinness's involvement, which they hoped would bring much-needed expertise. Patrick Berry of Caerau Progressive Club wondered if Harp thought the company could be successful? Mr Lipscomb confirmed that Harp 'considered the company viable provided the financial uncertainty was removed'.

Trevor Morgan of Tynewydd Labour Club referred to the fact that 'in 1919 there were seven clubs breweries but five of those have now closed'. He summed up the mood when he added: 'The company is fortunate to have the support of the Guinness group'. The necessary resolutions were passed with a 99 per cent majority in favour. Guinness was in the driving seat.

STOUT RESCUES

1990-1994

Gareth Thomas, Crown's departing managing director, said after the EGM: 'We would prefer this deal not to look like a rescue plan, but at the end of the day that is how it will look.' The question was, had the rescue come too late? The loss for the year to 30 September 1990 was again over £1 million.

New managing director Mike Salter later recalled: 'When I got here I found that the company was not looking very good. One only needs to glance at the annual report to see how bad the situation was. The business had suffered one blow after another. I think most of the staff and many customers were left shell-shocked by it all. The company had no clear sense of direction, no current marketing plans and no sense of corporate identity.'

But the new management had more muscle than the old. With Guinness in complete charge – the reformed board even appointed the stout brewer's secretary Brian Beanland as company secretary – Crown Buckley was placed on a sounder footing at the beginning of October when Guinness loaned the company the huge amount of £7 million at favourable rates to pay off all its debts and loans from the Midlands and Barclays banks. Crown Buckley's business assets and property were provided as security. New bankers, National Westminster, were appointed, and Crown adopted Guinness's auditors Price Waterhouse.

With the support of a major brewer, Crown Buckley was able to pay shareholders a dividend despite its heavy losses. And with the elimination of the loss-making activities of the London depot and the managed house section of Crown Buckley Taverns – managed houses were transferred to tenancies – and some unprofitable pubs sold or closed, the future looked much brighter. The conversion of the huge Harp debt to share capital also reduced the crippling interest rate burden.

Mike Salter's new management team examined every aspect of the company in detail. Immediate priorities included a new production and distribution plan, staff reorganization and new marketing plans. Visits were made to every pub and main club customers. Stricter financial controls were introduced. His executive meetings became the decision-making body within the company, with the board reduced to meeting once every two months.

However, the option of moving all operations to one site was not taken up, though the brewing vessels were still in place at Pontyclun. A visitor later recalled: 'The Pontyclun plant has the air of a ghost brewery, even two years after its closure. White brewers' coats still hang on the pegs where they were left. The fermenting vessels, coppers and mash tuns are still in place. "Grains in the mash tun are not to be touched until 1pm" says a dusty notice. They remain untouched.' Now new offices were built in part of the fermenting room.

Despite the CIU's refusal to allow their officer, Colin Hughes, to continue to sit on the board, Mike Salter was anxious to maintain close relations. He held meetings with the CIU nationally and in South Wales, where the company pledged its continuing support for the clubs movement to the extent of being 'prepared to place funds equivalent to the salaries previously paid to directors representing the CIU at the branch's disposal'. Eventually, early in 1991, a Supply and Distribution Committee was set up to which two representatives of the South Wales CIU were appointed.

Having worked for Britain's largest brewers, Bass, at the highest level, both in Cardiff and London, Mike Salter was perplexed by some of the goings-on at the clubs brewery. On one of his first days at Pontyclun he noticed a coach arrive and pull up at the side of the brewery early one morning. A large party tumbled out into the 'hatch', the room where staff often enjoyed a pint or three of free beer. On going to investigate, he discovered the visitors happily helping themselves. 'I was amazed,' he said. It seemed that club outings, off for a day at the races or on some other trip, regularly called in at the brewery for a morning freshener, before carrying on their way. Mike Salter politely asked the party to leave. The hatch was closed and staff instead provided with a monthly allowance of beer to take home. He also abandoned the previous practice of giving bottles of spirits to directors who attended meetings. On another occasion he complained about the state of the brewery yard and asked for it to be cleaned up. The next morning he turned up to find all the drays still at Pontyclun. Fearing a strike, he rushed to discover what was the problem. 'We're tidying the yard, like you asked,' he was told. Mike Salter ordered the fleet out. 'Customer deliveries come first.'

Improvement did not happen overnight. In fact for the last quarter of 1990, Crown Buckley lost a further £501,000, though this included an exceptional write down of stock of £173,000. Sales were still sliding. Total sales of 34,695 barrels for the quarter were 11.5 per cent below the same period the previous year, while costs were well over target.

Significantly, it was the weaker beers which suffered most. In December production of the once-popular CPA fell by a massive 62 per cent. Output collapsed from 1,031 barrels in the same month in 1989 to 390 barrels in December 1990. Brenin also fell by 29 per cent. The market was changing rapidly, with the sharp decline of the old heavy industries like mining and steel. However, sales of stronger beers held up well. The company began to look seriously at the question of producing a premium ale.

Prices were kept down during this period as it was felt 'tactically wrong' to put them up following the EGM. Buckley's Best Bitter was launched in cans in November, but too late to gain a Christmas listing with large supermarkets, Tesco and Gateway.

However, none of these immediate disappointments could dampen the new mood of optimism. Commercial director Phil Moore told the board in January 1991 that 'sales had picked up during the last two weeks of December, and with the sales force now working to clearly defined objectives and the new loan opportunities identified, he was confident that the company could improve its market share in 1991'.

The next month saw the first fruits of this new optimism, as Crown Buckley pushed into Brain's backyard in the centre of Cardiff. The clubs brewery was supporting a new restaurant, Yesterdays, within 500 yards of their rival's brewery. It was hoped that the backing would provide a better tomorrow. 'We hope Yesterdays will give us a springboard into Cardiff by catching the eye of publicans in the free trade and those in tied houses looking for guest ales,' said Mike Salter. This was followed in March by the start of a two-month £200,000 television and poster promotion for Buckley's Best Bitter, 'The Golden Oldie', in south-east Wales.

That month the company made a profit of £37,000 after a poor start to the year. The management team was also strengthened with the arrival of Richard Cunningham as operations director. A former colleague of Mike Salter, he had previously been a director of Bass Wales and West for ten years, and now made up a slimmed-down management team of four. Previously there had been ten. By May the monthly profit had increased to £89,000. Sales were still 10 per cent down on the previous year, but the company was more efficiently run.

The shrinking taverns division was merged with the free trade business in June. The number of pubs was down to under 100. That summer part of the distribution fleet was based at Llanelli to improve customer service in west Wales. This followed the closure of the Narberth depot. July was 'a good month for sales' with trade up 3 per cent on the previous year, though discounts hit profit margins.

Crown Buckley had been talking about providing a premium cask bitter for a number of months. Three options were considered: brewing their own; having one brewed by another brewery under Crown Buckley's name or selling a well-known beer like Marston's Pedigree, Ind Coope's Burton Ale or Felinfoel Double Dragon. In the end they decided to take the first option and brew their own. The name of the new ale came as a surprise to many drinkers. In a land where the pub and the chapel often stood uneasily side by side in the same street, the title seemed provocative. The premium beer was called Reverend James. It was named after Revd James Buckley, one of the founders of the Llanelli brewery which carries his name. Though a leading Methodist, he had no worries about owning a brewery when he inherited his father-in-law's business in 1824. The powerful temperance tradition of the Welsh chapels came later.

After a trial in twenty pubs, the strong 4.5 per cent beer, based on a recipe dating from the eighteenth century, was featured at CAMRA's beer festival in Cardiff in October before being launched early in November. 'The Reverend James completes our ale portfolio and complements Brenin and Buckley's Best Bitter, our two largest-selling brands,' said Mike Salter. 'We are confident that it will become the definitive premium cask-conditioned ale in South Wales.' The company also relaunched the low-gravity keg bitter, Brenin.

In November Gareth Thomas resigned as a director after fifteen years with the company, in order to set up his own wholesale beer business. He was replaced as chairman by Ivor Evans. The following month the restructuring of the company was completed. The pub properties were transferred to another group company, with Crown Buckley Taverns ceasing to trade. Crown Buckley would still supply all the beer and manage the houses. This transfer resulted in an exceptional gain of £1,691,000 – more than offsetting high interest charges for the year of over £1 million.

This meant Crown Buckley was able to declare a pre-tax profit for 1991 of £636,000. Without the exceptional gain, the company had made an operating loss for the year of

£15,000. Improved sales and efficiency had been offset by the cost of internal reorganization. But this small reverse was a major improvement on the last three months of 1990, when the trading loss was £247,000.

The directors were still optimistic. They stated in the annual report: 'Underlying trends in our trading show encouraging signs of progress. Increased marketing spend coupled with a loan investment programme has helped the company to gain market share and to maintain volumes in a declining market. After a poor start to the year our sales have out-performed the market and we have high hopes in 1992 of further growth.'

Mike Salter sounded bullish when he talked to CAMRA's newspaper *What's Brewing*. 'There is a lot of uncertainty among the major brewers following the MMC report [which stripped them of many of their pubs and allowed guest beers into their remaining houses]. This gives us an opportunity to establish ourselves as the regional brewer for South Wales.'

He particularly had his eye on Cardiff where Crown Buckley were now supplying the popular Chapter Arts Centre and the Sandringham Hotel. 'We have for too long been associated with clubs in the valleys and pubs in west Wales. We must mount a challenge in south-east Wales if we are to prosper.'

When the AGM was held in Port Talbot in March, Mike Salter forecast that the business would soon be back in the black. He praised the performance of Buckley's Best Bitter. Sales were up 35 per cent during 1991. Business was looking brighter. The company clinched a three-year sponsorship deal with Llanelli rugby club.

Crown Buckley might sound optimistic, but the question was how long Guinness would wait for success? The firm now had a £9.5m loan from Guinness, and the stout brewers were looking for some return on their massive investment. Early in 1992 James Barrett, seconded from auditors Price Waterhouse, replaced Tim Jones in the hot seat as finance director.

Sales for the first three months of 1992, while 4.3 per cent below those of the previous year, were 5.7 per cent above budget. The company was making progress on its planned path. Costs were kept tight. The bottling and kegging teams at Pontyclun were combined and the garage was closed with vehicle maintenance contracted out. A further six workers were made redundant.

By the August board meeting it was noted that 'there was no sign of any upturn in the current economic climate'. It was agreed that Mike Salter should 'review expenditure levels for the remainder of 1992 to see where savings could be achieved should sales continue at their current depressed levels for the remainder of the year'. One casualty was the cash and carry at Pontyclun. To add insult to injury £9,000 worth of spirits was stolen from the shop before closure.

Prices were increased by 3.8 per cent with a warning from chairman Ivor Evans that 'while he accepted the need for a price increase, many clubs would view the increases with concern'. He feared the rise could further depress sales. Agreement had been reached with wholesalers Steadmans of Newport to supply them with 1,000 barrels a year. But this positive development was soon soured by news that two other Welsh wholesalers had gone bankrupt, leaving the company with serious bad debts.

It was a depressing summer for Buckley's 225th anniversary celebrations. A special bottled brew of Reverend James was produced to mark the occasion and officially launched at the Llanelli brewery in September by MP Sir Wyn Roberts, the Welsh Office Minister of State. While everyone toasted the company's long past, rumours were already swirling around about its immediate future.

In February 1993 the issue broke into the open. The *Western Mail*'s business editor Neil Jones revealed that a management buyout was being seriously considered as 'Guinness sought to stem losses suffered by the South Wales business'. In 1992 the company had lost a further £266,000, with Guinness helping pay the dividend.

Two other options were also being examined, he said. The first was the closure of the Llanelli brewery with the loss of forty jobs, with Buckley's beers made elsewhere under contract. The other option was the sale of Crown Buckley to another brewery. The frontrunner was Ushers of Wiltshire.

Mike Salter refused to comment, but Guinness's public affairs director Bill Spears was more forthcoming. 'We have been working with the company's management to develop the business further. It must be remembered that we rescued the business in 1990 from near-certain oblivion when the banks had virtually pulled the plug.'

The annual directors' report for 1992, finally issued in May, highlighted the unsettling effect of the whirlwind of whispers whistling through many club committees and bars. 'It is extremely difficult to comment on the pattern of trade in 1992 without reference to the rumours about the future of the company that pervaded the market in the second half of the year. This uncertainty was exploited by our rivals.'

The board thanked 'the vast majority of shareholders, customers and employees who remained loyal and supportive through what was a most difficult period, so minimizing the damage to the company.' The directors added that 'the continuing special relationship between the company and its shareholders via the advisory committee has never been more evident. The board remains convinced that the existence and help of the advisory committee are a major benefit to both the company and the shareholders.'

The new management might owe their jobs and allegiance to Guinness, but they recognized that the historic links of the clubs brewery could even now provide a handsome dividend. Loyalty still paid.

The board meeting in April noted that 'it was essential that any management buyout was widely supported by clubs and shareholders.' Meetings were arranged at Brynamman Industrial, Penywaun Welfare, Penrhiwfer Social and Trefelin Workingmen's clubs. Chairman Ivor Evans said the shareholder representatives would support a management buyout 'provided this secured the long-term future of the brewery'.

The buyout was finally concluded in May after some fifteen months of

BLESSED BEER: *More promotion was put behind Crown Buckley's premium ale Reverend James after the management buyout*

negotiations, and officially announced on 1 June. Crown Buckley's senior management had bought Harp's 75 per cent share stake in the company with financial backing from Prudential Venture Managers and Barclays Bank. The sale involved the two sites and the rights to all the brands, with a pledge that brewing would continue at Llanelli, while Pontyclun would remain as the head office and packaging and distribution centre.

It did not include the eighty pubs which remained part of Harp. The buyout team, however, had negotiated a five-year supply and management deal for the houses and held first option on their sale. Finance had already been arranged to buy the core of the estate – and additional houses in south-east Wales. The aim was eventually to own around 120 pubs spread across South Wales.

It was a bold move by the management team of managing director Mike Salter, operations director Richard Cunningham, sales director Phil Moore and finance director James Barrett. And one which must have caused more than a few sleepless nights. The buyout was one of the largest to take place in Wales. Despite increasing market share, trade was still well below target in a depressed market. Sales in March of around 9,000 barrels was almost 9 per cent below budget. The loss for the first three months was £357,000. The overdraft was over £9m.

'We have all had to put money in, and I am not entirely sure that our wives are happy

THE BUYOUT TEAM: Mike Salter is left holding the cans watched by (left to right) James Barrett, Richard Cunningham and Phil Moore

about us securing our houses on the future of a brewery,' said Mike Salter. The men from the multi-nationals were now running their own local company.

A major motivating factor was the fear that all the hard work since 1990 would be thrown away if another company came along and closed the brewery. Ushers of Trowbridge in Wiltshire had been in the running. 'It was an emotional response. We wanted to see the rescue through. We did not want to see all our efforts wasted.'

Another vital factor was that Guinness agreed to remove the huge debt burden still crippling the company. A letter from financial consultants Touche Ross to shareholders stated: 'As part of this restructuring, Guinness has agreed to forgo a significant amount of the debt owing to it.' The company was left with a debt level it could afford.

The deal was approved by a special shareholders EGM held in the clubs brewery's heartland at Penygraig Labour Club in the Rhondda on 12 June. The support was crucial as the free trade still made up the bulk of Crown Buckley's business. Despite the change of ownership, a clubs committee continued to advise the new company. 'This is not a gesture to the past but an important working relationship,' stressed Mike Salter. 'They tell us what is happening in the clubs and help us make informed decisions.'

The chairman of the new company was announced as David Inns, a former finance director of Bass. The Prudential, who had supplied much of the capital, also gained a seat on the board. 'The negotiations were very intensive and absorbed all our attention. We did not see much of the business during that period,' admitted Mike Salter. 'I am looking forward to getting out and getting on with running a brewery again. We will not be trying to compete head on with the national brewers. We believe there is a market for a regional brewer offering local products and a local service.

'We like the more personal, almost family touch here,' he added about the company employing 175 workers. Earlier that year he had made presentations to nineteen employees with a total of 610 years service between them.

'We are indulging in our dreams. But we are determined to make it work.'

INDEX

Aberaman Ex-servicemen's Club 77
Aberavon 7, 80
Aberavon WMC 29, 63, 87, 105
Aberbeeg 90
Abercwmboi British Legion 98
Abercynon Ex-servicemen's Club 64
Aberdare 94
Aberfan 82
Abergwynfi Conservative Club 7
Abertillery 35, 111
Adlam & Sons 31, 40
Allbright 109, 111
Allied Breweries 86, 98, 109, 132, 134
Alloa 21
Alnwick 23
Amber Ale 83
Ammanford Social Club 60
Ansells 86, 98, 132, 133, 134
Antigallican, Charlton 117
Association of Clubs Breweries 39, 57, 63, 64, 82

B&Q 131
Badman, Charles 93
Baillie, Frank 103
Bairds 74
Baldock, Brian 132
Ball, D.G. 39, 49, 62, 66, 67, 81
Balsall Heath Labour Club 97
Banbury 18
Bank of Wales 124
Banks of Wolverhampton 124
Barclays Bank 137, 142
Barlow-Clowes 124
Barnard Castle 75
Barrett, James 140, 142
Barry 7
Barry Dock Liberal Club 29
Bass 13, 23, 31
Bass-Charrington 86, 87, 98, 138, 143
Basson, A.E. 56
Bass-Wales 135, 139
Bath 76
Batley WMC 4

Bay View Social Club 77, 121
Beanland, Brian 137
Bedwas WMC 50, 77
Beer Drinkers' Companion 103
Beer Duty 29, 33, 35, 36, 50, 52, 87
Beer Gravity 13, 21, 29, 33, 34, 36, 50, 52, 53, 54, 61, 62, 64, 65, 83, 115, 120
Beer is Best 5
Beer Mats 37
Beer Prices 9, 13, 32, 33, 50, 52, 55, 61, 64, 65, 66, 77, 81, 82, 83, 88, 94, 98, 113, 129, 140
Beer Quality 18, 54, 57, 59, 61, 62, 63, 64, 65, 71, 72–74, 128
Beethoven, Maesteg 117
Berry, Patrick 136
Berry, Sam 108
Berry, Sidney 60
Bevan, Gilbert 107
Birkbeck, Dr. 1
Birmingham 97, 98, 102
Blackpool 122
Black Prince 115, 127
Blackwells 34
Blackwood 24, 35, 111
Blaengarw Constitutional Club 7
Blaenllechau 32, 45
Blandford Forum, Dorset 38
Blyth, Danny 116
Board of Trade 55
Bonus 30, 34, 36, 37, 40, 54, 55, 56, 57, 59, 61, 62, 63, 64, 68, 77, 92, 96, 98, 111, 112
Bottled Beer 23, 32, 33, 36, 38, 49, 52, 57, 58, 73, 83, 88, 90, 94, 95, 96, 114, 115, 117, 122
Bowerman, C.W. 25
Bradford 16
Brain, Samuel 6
Brain, W.H. 29
Brain's Brewery 109, 138
Braunston WMC 100
Brecon 92
Brenin Bitter 111, 113, 114, 115, 117, 122, 127, 128, 130, 138, 139
Brewers' Exhibition 83, 103, 114, 116

INDEX

Brewers' Journal 10, 13, 16, 17, 28, 42, 43
Brewers' Society 36
Brewery extensions 40, 41, 49, 59, 60, 61, 63
Brewing Industry International Awards 122
Bridges, C.W. 81, 82, 102
Briggs of Burton on Trent 40, 56, 59
Bristol 76, 112
Brithdir Ex-Servicemen's Club 29
Bromley Common Social Club 117
Bromsgrove Labour Club 97
Brougham, Lord 2
Brown, John 67, 81
Brown Bracer 32, 52, 83, 97
Brunel Arms, Pontyclun 117, 118
Brynamman Industrial Club 64, 142
Buchan, Andrew of Rhymney 58
Buckley, Revd James 139
Buckley, Kemmis 124
Buckley's Best Bitter 127, 128, 129, 131, 138, 139, 140
Buckley's Brewery 32, 109, 124–128, 132, 135, 140, 141
Burnham, Somerset 18
Burnley Clubs Brewery 16
Burton Ale 139
Burton on Trent 122, 124
Button, Ian 107

Caerau Progressive Club 64, 77, 105, 136
Caernarfon, Lord 4
Caerphilly 132
Caerphilly Social Club 45
Cambrian Colliery Disaster 82
CAMRA 103, 116, 139, 140
Cannock 97
Cardiff 6, 7, 9, 10, 21, 41, 42, 60, 66, 94, 103, 109, 126, 138, 139, 140
Cardiff Arms Park 126
Cardiff Royal Infirmary 56
Carling Black Label 82, 90
Carlisle 8
Carlsberg 94, 121
Carmarthen 92, 112
Cathays Liberal Club 9, 28
Cefn Viaduct Brewery 21, 25
Celtic Bright 128
Celtic Club 62
Chapman, Mr. 39, 60
Chapter Arts Centre 140
Charles Barker, Black & Gross 102
Charlton 116
Charrington United Breweries 82

Christmas Bonus 18, 29, 30, 90, 117
Christmas Gifts 53, 76, 85
Churchill, Winston 53
CIU 2–8, 9, 10, 16, 18, 21, 25–27, 29, 35, 36, 39, 40, 43–45, 51, 53, 60, 64, 66, 69, 80, 82, 86, 87, 93, 97, 105, 115, 120, 122, 135, 138
Clark, George & Son 36
Clark, Peter G. 53, 61, 67, 86, 89, 97, 102, 111
Clowes, Peter 124
Club Brew 33, 52
Club Journal 6, 33, 36, 40, 43, 44, 97, 98
Club Special 52, 58, 83, 95
Club Symbol 40
Club Union Convalescent Homes 77
Clubs Amber 95
Clubs Breweries Federation 24, 33, 39
Clubs Brown 95
Clubs Extra 95
Clubs Pale Ale 10, 103
Clubs Registration Bill 49
Clydach Vale 64
Clydach Vale WMC 83
Coca-Cola 122
Coleford 92
Colliers Arms, Blackwells 34
Collins, Frank 67
Conservative Party 7
Cooperative Bank 68
Cooperative Club 121
Cotterell, O.E. 97
Courage 86, 124, 125
Coventry 99
Cowbridge 9
Cox, David 111, 114
CPA 10, 32, 33, 50, 59, 62, 77, 83, 88, 94, 103, 111, 115, 138
Cramer, Guy Von 124
Crenigan, Phil 136
Crone, J.A. 67
Crosswells Brewery 30
Crown-Buckley 121, 125–143
Crown Keg 96, 99, 109, 110, 111, 128
Crown Sparkler 32, 33, 52
Crown Taverns 121
Crumlin WMC 19
Culverwell, Mr. 59, 60, 61, 63, 64, 65, 66, 67, 76
Cunningham, Richard 139, 142
Cwm WMC 35
Cymmer Pioneer Club 34

Daily Mirror 50
Darbyshire, T. 59, 60, 63

INDEX

Dark Mild 109, 115
Davies, Arthur 67, 81, 86, 87, 102, 105
Davies, Ben 27
Davies, C.J. 81, 102
Davies, Denzil, MP 131
Davies, E.T. 51
Davies, Lord Elfed 105
Davies, George 18, 19, 21, 24, 25, 28, 35, 45, 50
Davies, J.P. 9, 10, 21, 28, 45, 51, 57, 64, 65
Davies, John 106
Defence of the Realm Act 8
Devenish Brewery, Weymouth 30
Dickens, Charles 1
Discounts 18, 28, 33
Dormer, Jack 115
Double Diamond 86, 97
Double Dragon 139
Double Six 83
Douglas, James 67
Druids 1
Drybrough of Edinburgh 90
Durham 16

Ebbw Vale Council of Clubs 82
Edwards, Frank 67
Elders 124
Evan Bevan's Bitter 85
Evan Evans Bevan of Neath 76, 86–87
Evans, Barry 108
Evans, Ceri 96, 97, 105, 106, 107
Evans, David 67, 68
Evans, Ivor 139, 140, 142
Evans, Penri 64, 69, 72, 77, 81, 86, 90, 92, 96, 97, 102, 105, 106, 107, 108
Exeter 112
Extra Strong Pale Ale 83

Farmers Arms, Glyncorrwg
Felinfoel 109, 139
Ferndale 10
Ferndale Imperial Club 112
Fernvale 82
Fernvale Brewery 86, 87
Fishguard & Goodwick Railwaymen's Club 45
Fleur-de-Lis 23, 24
Forest of Dean 76
Fosters 124
Furniture & Equipment Supplies (Pontyclun) Ltd 80

Gaskell, Col. J.G. 65
Gateway 138
Gell, Tom 44

General Strike (1926) 29
Gilbert, J.D. 67
Gilfach Goch Conservative Club 93
Gilfach Goch Ex-Servicemen's Club 93
Gilfach Goch Festival Club 93
Gilfach Goch Social Club 92, 93, 96
Gladstone, William 2
Glamorgan Gazette 103
Glanville, A.P. 67, 81
Glovers of Neath 31
Glyncoch Social Club 136
Glyncoed Social Club 90
Glyncorrwg 34
Golden Jubilee Booklet 72
Great Western 103, 107–108, 111, 114, 120
Great Western Railway 23
Greenall Whitley 135
Greene King 131
Greenlands Social Club 97
Gretton, Col. 13
Griffiths, W. 51, 60
Guinness 23, 31, 32, 66, 72, 73, 82, 102, 125, 128, 129, 131–138, 140, 141, 143
Gurnos Estate 80
Gwent Union Clubs Brewery 23–25
Gwyn Davies, Maj. E. 67

Hall, B.T. 4
Hall, Malcolm 131–132
Hall, Syd 19, 21
Hambleton, L. 63, 88, 94
Hamill Toms 111
Hampshire 97
Hancock's Brewery 35, 65, 86, 87, 88
Harp 82, 96, 102, 109, 114, 117, 120, 121, 122, 124, 125, 126, 131, 132, 133, 135, 136, 142
Haverfordwest 112
Heineken 125
Heycock, E. 29, 34, 39
Hick's Brewery, St. Austell 21
Hobbes, Mr. & Mrs. 65
Hobbs, Frank 67
Hoddlesden, Lancs 4
Hofmeister 125
Holt Brothers 18
Honorbrook Inns 112
Hopkinstown Non-Political Club 54
Hospital Fund 56
Howe, H. 9, 10, 18, 19
Huddersfield 18
Hughes, Colin 105, 106, 107, 112, 122, 132, 135, 138
Hughes, Rodger 132

INDEX

IBA 109
Ind Coope 86, 139
Inns, David 143
Insolvency Act 132
Ivor Arms, Brynsadler 9, 10

James, Dan 18, 49, 51, 53, 54, 56, 57, 60, 62
JB 128
Jeffrey, Don 126, 127
Jenkins, D. & T. Ltd 9–15
Jenkins, David 9, 18, 19
Jenkins, Gareth 126
Jenkins, Thomas 9
Jenks, Mr 39
Johnson, Brian 131
Johnson, Dr. Samuel 1
Jones, D. 19
Jones, D.J. 32
Jones, Denzil 106, 107, 112, 113, 115, 117, 120, 121, 123, 125, 128, 131, 135, 136
Jones, L.C. 33
Jones, Neil 141
Jones, Tim 126, 128, 132, 133, 140
Jones, Tom 51
Jones. W. 51

Keg Beer 86, 88, 89, 94, 96, 99, 102, 103, 107, 108, 109, 114, 115, 116, 117, 128
King George V 103
Kinsman, J.W. 7, 9, 18, 32, 38, 39, 56, 92
Knight, John 109
Kronenbourg 109

Labour Exchange 54
Lancashire Clubs Brewery 69, 83
Landeg, Jack 45
Langland Bay Home 7, 25, 26
Langland Bay Hotel 25, 36, 40, 49, 50, 53, 54, 59, 62, 64, 65, 76
Lavers, Sidney 72, 74, 75
Law Reform Society 106
Leeds & District Clubs Brewery 16
Leicester 2, 16, 61, 97
Leominster Trades & Social Club 97
Leyshon, R.G. 81, 90
Liberal Party 7
Lipscomb, Peter 133, 134, 136
Llanbradach Social Club 45
Llandilo 16
Llanelli 94, 124, 125, 126, 127, 131, 132, 139, 141, 142
Llanelli Rugby Club 140

Llantrisant 9, 10, 54, 117
Llantrisant & Llantwit Pardre Rural Council 67
Llantrisant Rd 74
Llantwit Major Social Club 45
Lloyd George, David 7, 8, 21, 28
Local Veto 3, 28
London 42, 115, 120, 121, 131
London Bier Keller 117
Long, Ray 106, 113, 117
Lougher, David 81, 115, 122
Lynvi Valley Social Club 117
Lyttleton, Lord 2

MacDonald, Ramsey 25
MacKenzie, John 67
Mackeson 97
Maesteg 94
Maesteg Catholic Club 30
Maesteg WMC 60
Mardy Social Club 82
Mardy Workmen's Hall 82
Marsh, Lee 38, 40, 41, 50, 51, 53, 54, 56, 57, 58, 62, 64, 72, 73, 74, 81, 83, 85, 86, 88
Marston's, Burton on Trent 124
Marston's Pedigree 139
Marxian WMC 72
McEnery, Mr 66
Mechanics Institutes 1
Medway Federation of Clubs Brewery 16, 31
Mendip Brewery 112
Merthyr Express 1
Merthyr Tydfil 1, 6, 21, 25, 80, 94
Merthyr Tydfil Labour Club 60
Metropolitan & Home Counties Clubs Brewery 64, 83
Midland Bank 68, 80, 98, 125, 129, 132, 134, 137
Midlands Clubs Brewery 97
Mid-Rhondda Central 96
Mild, 127
Ministry of Food 55, 59, 61, 63, 66
Ministry of Transport 76
Ministry of Works 59, 60, 61
Mitchell's & Butler's 98
Mogg, W.G. (Billy) 93
Moore, Philip 135, 138, 142
Mordecai, Danny 107, 108
Morgan, E. 74
Morgan, Grenfell 124
Morgan, John Ltd 66, 67, 69
Morgan, T. 107
Morgan, Thomas 7
Morgan, Trevor 136
Morgan, W. 51, 60, 62, 64, 67

INDEX

Morning Advertiser 65
Morris, Hopkins 27
Mountain Ash Hibernia 33
Mountain Ash WMC 18
Mumbles Lifeboat 62
Murison, Mrs 25, 36, 65
Murphys of St. Albans 40

Narberth 112, 128, 131, 139
National Westminster Bank 137
Neath 31
Neath Central Club 90
New Brewery 61, 62, 63, 64, 65, 66–71, 72, 76, 80, 81
Newcastle 16, 23, 61, 74, 104
New Inn 65
New Park Liberal Club 21, 28
Newport 33, 94, 111, 132
Nichols, Beverly 45
North of England Clubs Brewery 16
Northampton WMC 4
Northants & Leicester 69
Northern Clubs Federation Brewery 16, 23, 67, 74, 75, 83, 99, 102, 104, 109, 115, 166, 120, 122

Oddfellows 1
Old Fox, Bristol 103
Oldham, Chris 126
Olympia 83, 86
Oystermouth Social Club 62

PA 33, 50, 61
Park Royal Brewery 120
Pearce, A. 9, 19
Pearce, H.J. 51, 64, 65, 66, 67, 71, 73, 74, 76
Peart, Fred MP 92
Penn, T. 67
Penrhiwceiber British Legion 59, 64
Penrhiwfer Social Club 142
Pentrebach Labour Club 77
Penygraig Labour Club 45, 48, 77, 143
Penywaun Welfare Club 142
Phillips, Miss 38
Phillips, Griff 29
Phillips, T.H. 32
Phipps of Northampton 90
Plastishield 114
Pontyclun Social Club 51, 117, 118, 119
Pontygwaith 82
Pontypridd 7, 10, 19, 21, 39, 62, 64, 111
Portmead Social Club 98
Porth 51, 117
Porthcawl 45, 56

Port Talbot 33, 77, 120, 121, 140
Port Talbot Labour Club 117, 119
Post-War Plant Committee 56
Pratt, Hodgson 4
Price Waterhouse 137, 140
Prince of Wales 2
Prohibition 3, 7, 10, 28
Project Yellow 125
Prosser, Port Talbot 33, 34
Prudential, The 143
Prudential Venture Managers 142
Pubs 34, 82, 102, 103, 112, 116, 117, 121, 124, 139, 142

Rainton 16
Rationing 53, 54, 60, 62, 63, 65
Randall's Brewery, Guernsey 114
Reading 112
Real Ale 102–103, 115, 116, 120
Red Barrel 86, 89, 90
Redditch 97
Rees, Evan 33, 60, 67, 72, 74
Rees, Jim 131, 136
Reverend James 139, 140, 141
Rhondda Champagne 115
Rhondda Sports Centre 135
Rhondda Valley 9, 10, 36, 45, 48, 94
Rhondda Valley Brewery 23, 24
Rhydyfelin Labour Club 106
Rhymney Brewery 30, 82, 86–87
Rhymney WMC 44
Rich, Tom 9, 10, 19, 33, 51
Richards, Huw 9, 10, 21, 24, 27, 28, 29, 32, 35, 36, 37, 38, 39, 40, 51
Risca 10, 23
Roberts, Sir Wyn 140
Rogers, Albert George 35
Rogers, Capt. W.J. 10, 21, 38, 56
Rossiter, Fred 67
Rowe, Bertie 51, 53, 64, 72, 74, 76, 80, 81, 82, 86
Rowson, Mr. 32
Royal Commission on Licensing (1931) 16, 27, 42
Royal Commission on Sunday Closing (1889) 6
Royal Mint, Llantrisant 117

St. Austell, Cornwall 21
St. Helens 89
St. Oswalds 117, 119
St. Oswalds Special 120
Salter, Mike 135, 136, 137, 138, 139, 140, 141, 142, 143
Same Again 109, 111

INDEX

Samuel, Gary 126
Sandfields 80
SBB 77, 83–85, 88, 97, 103, 111, 115, 116, 117, 121
Schweppes 122
Scottish & Newcastle 86, 96, 132, 134
Shebeens 6–7
Singer & Friedlander 124
Six Bells 82
Skinner, L.R. 40
Skol 109
Smith, Bob 89, 114, 116, 120, 126
Solly, Henry 2, 4
Southampton 97
South Wales Bottlers' Association 56, 82
South Wales Brewers' Association 20, 21, 96, 102
South Wales Echo 35, 94
South Wales Trade Defence League 29
South-West Midlands Clubs Association 97
Sovereign 96, 98, 99
Spears, Bill 141
Special 58
Spitfire Fund 52
Star Brewery, Slaithwaite 16
Star Inn, Treoes 117, 118
Star Special 120
Steadmans of Newport 140
Stephen, G. 81
Sunday Chronicle 45, 48
Sunday Closing 29, 45
Sunday Closing (Wales) Act 6, 7, 45
Sunderland 16
Swansea 6–7, 25, 53, 62, 94, 109, 111
Swansea Valley 82, 96
Swindon 76

Taf Fechan Water Board 102
Taff Ely 114
Taff Vale Railway 18
Taibach 29, 34
Taibach WMC 77
Talfan Davies, Sir Alun 124
Tarbuck, Jimmy 113
Taylor of Treforest 69
Taylor, Alan 93
Taylor, Teddy 82
Temperance Movement 1–5, 28, 139
Temperance (Wales) Bill 28
Tenby 112
1041 (Ten forty-one) 122, 128
Tesco 138
Tetleys 86
TGWU 131

Thatcher, Maggie 113
Thomas, Gareth 107, 113, 125, 126, 128, 131, 132, 133, 134, 135, 136, 137, 139
Thomas, Haydn 32
Thomas, Sir Percy 66
Thomastown Social Club 131
Thornycroft lorries 78
Tied-House System 16
Times, The 7
Ton Pentre 32
Ton Pentre Club 18
Ton Pentre Labour Club 64, 72
Tonyrefail Non-Political Club 77
Touche Ross 143
Trebanog WMC 51
Trefelin WMC 142
Treoes 117, 118, 120
Treorchy Social Club 77
Triple Crown 83, 97
Tuborg 94–95, 96
Tuborg Pilsner 109
Tuborg Gold 109
Tylorstown 88
Tylorstown WMC 62, 107
Tynewydd Labour Club 136

United Clubs Brewery Stakes 103
Uplands WMC 72, 74
Upper Rhondda 64
Usher's Brewery, Wiltshire 90, 121, 122, 141, 143

Vale of Neath Brewery 76
Vaughan, H. 51
VE Day 58
VJ Day 59
Visits to brewery 27, 33

Wages Disputes 19–21
Walsall 98
Walton, E. 51
War Risks Insurance 49, 54
Warrington 135
Watney, Combe, Reid 36
Watney Mann 36, 90, 92, 98, 104, 121
Watson, Mr 53
Webbs 82, 86, 87, 90
Weekly Dispatch 13
Wellington, J. 81
Welsh Brewers 87, 109, 111
Welsh Mid-District Rugby Union 102
Western Mail 67, 77, 107, 109, 125, 131, 141
West Midlands Clubs Brewery 24

INDEX

What's Brewing 116, 140
Whiffs 54
Whitbread 86–87, 97, 117, 124, 125
Whitbread Tankard 86
Whitbread Wales 87
Wilcocks, Michael 124
Willenhall 24
Williams, Bryn 67
Williams, E.O. 51
Williams, James 112
Williams, Trevor 39, 51, 56, 57, 58, 59, 61, 62, 64, 65, 66, 69, 73, 76
Wilsons of Manchester 90
Wingfield Digby, Stephen 125, 132, 134, 136
Wolverhampton 24, 124
Woolton, Lord 55

Worthington 31, 32
Worthington, E. 86
Wrexham Lager Beer Co. 40

XXX 33, 50, 59, 61
XXXX 10, 32, 33, 50, 62, 77, 83

Yesterdays 139
Ynysddu WMC 21
Ynyshir WMC 63
York 61
Yorkshire Clubs Brewery 31, 97, 99
Yorkshire Post 16, 29
Younger's Tartan 96
Younger, George 21
Ystrad Rhondda 135